ORIGINAL PAPERS

RELATIVE TO

TANJORE

ORIGINAL PAPERS
RELATIVE TO
TANJORE:

CONTAINING ALL THE

LETTERS Which Passed, and the CONFERENCES Which were held, between his Highness the Nabob of ARCOT and GEORGE PIGOT, on the Subject of the Restoration of Tanjore.

GYAN

Published by

Gyan Publishing House
5, Ansari Road
Daryaganj, New Delhi-110002
Phone: 011-47034999, 9811692060
E-mail: books@gyanbooks.com

Distribution Network
gyanbooks.com
India, USA, Canada, UK, Australia, France

ISBN : 978-81-212-9096-8 (PB)
First Published, 1777

2nd Impression 2023

Printed at: Gyan Press, Delhi.

ORIGINAL PAPERS RELATIVE TO TANJORE
AUTHOR: LORD PIGOT

ORIGINAL PAPERS

RELATIVE TO

TANJORE.

ORIGINAL PAPERS

RELATIVE TO

TANJORE:

CONTAINING ALL THE

LETTERS which passed, and the CONFERENCES which were held, between his Highness the Nabob of ARCOT and Lord PIGOT, on the Subject of the Restoration of TANJORE.

TOGETHER WITH

The material Part of LORD PIGOT's last Dispatch to the EAST INDIA COMPANY.

The Whole connected by a NARRATIVE, and illustrated with NOTES and OBSERVATIONS.

LONDON:
PRINTED FOR T. CADELL, IN THE STRAND.
MDCCLXXVII.

ADVERTISEMENT.

THE following collection contains all the letters which passed, and the conferences which were held, between his Highness the Nabob of Arcot and Lord Pigot, on the subject of the restoration of Tanjore, to the displaced Raja. Most of the papers were transmitted by the Nabob, by a special messenger in a French ship, which left Pondicherry in the end of July last; and the remainder consists of the *material part* of Lord Pigot's dispatch to the East-India Company, by the same vessel.

To render the subject more intelligible to the reader, the papers are connected by a narrative and illustrated with notes. An INTRODUCTION is prefixed, explaining the right of the Nabob to Tanjore; and OBSERVATIONS are annexed to the whole, which, it is hoped, contain a COMPLETE REFUTATION of such arguments, as are advanced by the adherents of Lord Pigot, and the authors of the unjust and impolitic orders, for the restoration of Tanjore. Nothing, in short, has been omitted, that was thought conducive to the throwing light on a subject, which must come under public discussion, on account of its own importance, and the flagrant injustice of the East-India Company's servants.

INTRODUCTION*.

THE flagrant acts of injustice committed by the EAST-INDIA COMPANY, as well as by their *servants*, against the natives of India, have always called forth the *pity*, and sometimes the *animadversion* of the nation. At present, the *attention* of the public, and (it is to be hoped) its *resentment*, are rouzed by the unheard-of oppressions heaped upon *Mahommed Ali*, NABOB of ARCOT, the old, faithful, and strenuous ally of the British nation. The catalogue of the grievances of that unfortunate prince would fill a large volume; but we shall, at present, confine ourselves to the affair of TANJORE, in which the COMPANY's Servants have not only violated the *Rights* of the *Nabob*, but have even broken and trampled under foot the *Treaties* and most *solemn Engagements* of the *British Nation*.

Mahommed Ali, Nabob of *Arcot*, or the *Carnatic*, is descended from an ancient family, who accompanied the first Mogul conquerors into India, and who were eminent in the favour and service of the emperors of the Mogul race, ever since they established themselves on the throne of Delhi, in the year 1526. *Anwar*, the grandfather of the present Nabob, whilst

* A *State of Facts relative to Tanjore*, with an *Appendix* of *Original Papers*, was published, before the papers, which chiefly form this collection, were received from India. The *Facts*, contained in the *State*, are briefly recapitulated in this Introduction, with a design of throwing the *whole subject*, at once, before the eye of the reader. The *argument* is stated, with greater precision, in the OBSERVATIONS annexed to the papers; and *objections* are eithe *obviated* or *refuted*.

 Dur-

Dewan of the province of Patna, entered into the ſtricteſt friendſhip with the Engliſh nation. His father, *Anwar-ul-dien*, having obtained the Nabobſhip of Arcot, in the year 1744, uniformly ſided with the Engliſh againſt the French, till he was killed in battle by the latter, on the 23d of July 1749, bravely fighting for his allies and friends.

The preſent Nabob ſucceeded his father, in his affection for the Engliſh as well as in his government. He had done them the moſt eſſential ſervices, when his father was alive; he *ſaved* them, in a manner, from deſtruction, after his father's death. He ſupported the whole expence of the war on the coaſt of Coromandel; he advanced money for the expedition to Calcutta, which procured for us the kingdom of Bengal; he defrayed the expence of the ſiege of Pondicherry, and thus broke the power of the *French* in Hindoſtan. The friends of the Engliſh were his friends; he made their enemies his own; he communicated with them in all his councils; he made them partners in his authority, his power, and his reſources.

In return for theſe favours and ſervices, he was declared, in the *eleventh* article of the treaty of Paris, *lawful Nabob* of the *Carnatic*, and conſequently *Sovereign* and *feudal Lord* of TANJORE; a province in the very heart of the *Carnatic*, and ever ſince the Mogul conqueſt, uniformly *dependent* upon it. In addition to this ſolemn inveſtiture, by two of the greateſt nations in the world, the Mogul emperor, *Shah Allum*, by a Firmaun, dated in the year 1765, rendered him *independent* on the crown of Delhi.

Tanjore, before the conqueſt of it by the Moguls, was governed by its *native* princes, who became Zemindars or vaſſals to the conquerors. One of theſe princes, being preſſed by his neighbours, about eighty years ago, imprudently called to his aid a *Marattoe plunderer*, named *Eckogee*, who, with a perfidy common to his nation, ſeized *Tanjore*, and drove into exile the unfortunate man, to whoſe aſſiſtance he came. Eckogee and his family governed Tanjore, ever ſince, with the cruelty and ferocity natural to their race.

The Mogul emperors, as long as the tribute was paid, gave little attention to the title or inherent right of the Renter. They, however, augmented the tribute to *thirty lacks* per ann. which ſum was always paid to the Nabob of Arcot,

Arcot, within whose government Tanjore was always considered to lie. After several assassinations, one *Pertaub Sing*, a *bastard*, of the family of the usurper *Eckogee*, took possession of Tanjore in the year 1741. This perfidious tyrant, being execrated by the public, Ali Doost Chân, *Nabob of Arcot*, imprisoned him, upon an allowance of *half a crown* a day, to the great joy of the people of *Tanjore*. *Pertaub Sing*, however, upon the death of Ali Doost, in the year 1744, obtained the Zemindary, upon engaging to pay annually *fifty lacks* of rupees, or *six hundred and twenty-five thousand* pounds STERLING.

His former misfortunes produced no favourable effect on the treacherous mind of *Pertaub Sing*. When his *feudal Lord*, the present Nabob's father, was strenuously fighting for the *English*, this *vassal* avowedly aided the *French*. When *Anwar-ul-dien* was killed, by the *French*, on the 23d of July 1749, the hands of his son and successor, the *unfortunate prince* whom the East-India Company now *oppress*, were so much weakened, that he could not enforce the obedience of his vassal, *Pertaub Sing*; and the consequence was, that he refused to furnish his quota, for the defence of the country, against the *French* and *their allies*.

Notwithstanding a conduct so hostile to the *English*, and to their faithful ally, *Mr.* (now Lord) *Pigot*, concluded a treaty with *Pertaub Sing*, in direct violation of the *just rights* of his *feudal Lord*. *Pertaub Sing*'s tribute was reduced to little more than *forty thousand pounds* per ann.; a small sum was taken, in the place of all arrears, though Mr. Pigot had given the most *solemn assurances* to the *Nabob*, that he would assist him to recover the former tribute. A debt of seven lacks, (about *seventy-five thousand* pounds) for which *Pertaub Sing* had given his bond to the *Nabob*'s father, was declared to be cancelled. In vain did the unfortunate Nabob remonstrate against the *negociating* away his undoubted rights. A tributary Zemindar, or Renter, who had abetted the *French*, is placed by an *English governor* on the same footing with an *English ally*, an old, tried, and faithful friend. This unfortunate friend had his troops cut off on various occasions, his country depopulated, his revenues exhausted in fighting *our* battles. But, as his treasury was empty, he could not *purchase* even JUSTICE; but *Pertaub Sing*, having *not* done his duty, was in a condition to *obtain favours*. The remonstrances

monſtrances * of the *poor* Nabob were, therefore, loſt on the preſidency of Madras; for their *hearts* had been turned into *ſtones* †.

Soon after the concluſion of this *juſt* and *honourable* treaty, Iſouf Cawn, a ſubject of the Nabob, rebelled in the province of Madura. *Pertaub Sing* aided his rebellion with his councils, treaſure, and troops ‡; and, upon *Pertaub Sing*'s death, his ſon *Tuljagee*, the now reſtored Zemindar of *Tanjore*, ſucceeded him in his government, profligacy, and inveterate enmity to the *Engliſh* and the *Nabob*. He entered into a cloſe connection with *Iſouf Cawn* §, and afterwards with *Hyder Ali*; he aided that indefatigable partizan in invading the Carnatic. He gave him money, elephants, and proviſions; he enabled him, in ſhort, to puſh the war to the very gates of Madras ‖. Upon every occaſion he *inſulted* the *Engliſh* and the *Nabob*. Contrary to the remonſtrances of *both*, he invaded the territories of their vaſſals, he plundered the country, and turned, with the utmoſt indignity, their agents from his preſence ‡.

This hoſtile and unjuſt conduct muſt, in its very nature, have cancelled the treaty of 1762, had even that treaty been founded on *juſtice*: beſides, the treaty had expired with *Pertaub Sing*. Neither that Zemindar nor his ſon *Tuljagee* conſidered the treaty *perpetual*. It would not, in fact, be *perpetual*, as the *election* of the ſon was *eventual*, and de-

* Vide his letter to Mr. Pigot, of the 17th of July 1762, printed (p. 109.) in the following Collection.

† The treaty of Sept. 20th, 1762, is critically examined in the Obſervations annexed to theſe papers; which renders it unneceſſary to enlarge upon it, in this place.

‡ Vide an original letter from Pertaub Sing, Raja of Tanjore, to Iſouf Cawn, and two letters from Iſouf Cawn to Pertaub Sing, printed No. III. of the *State of Facts relative to Tanjore*, p. 46, 47, 48.

§ Vide two original letters from *Iſouf Cawn* to Tuljagee; and a letter from Monſieur Merchant to Tuljagee, on the ſame ſubject; printed in the Appendix to the *State relative to Tanjore*, No. III. p. 49, 50.

‖ Vide two original letters from Tuljagee to Hyder Ali, printed in the Appendix to the *State of Facts*, No. IV. p. 50, 51, 52.

‡ Vide Conſultations at Madras in 1768 and 1769, and general letters during thoſe two years. India-houſe. Conſultations, Feb. 11, 1771.

pended

pended on the favour and pleaſure of the *feudal ſuperior*, the *Nabob* of *Arcot*.

But ſhould it be granted, contrary to every idea of *juſtice*, and oppoſition to *truth* itſelf, that the treaty was *perpetual*, muſt the *Engliſh* and their ally, the *Nabob*, be precluded from enforcing * the *performance* of an obligation by which they themſelves are bound? Muſt they be *bound*, and *Tuljagee* be left at *liberty?* Does the *infamous* and *unjuſt* treaty of 1762 prohibit the Nabob from removing his *vaſſal* (even acknowledged as *ſuch* by *Lord Pigot* himſelf †) upon his failing to perform his *feudal duties?* Was not his father removed by a Subadâr of the Carnatic? Shall the *preſent Nabob* FORFEIT his rights for his alliance with the *Engliſh*; for his being *guaranteed* by the treaty of Paris; for his being declared *independent* of the empire of the Moguls? Shall every thing that eſtabliſhed the *rights* of other princes, deprive the *unfortunate* MAHOMED ALI of *his* rights, becauſe his ſituation has placed him within the *reach* of the *inſatiable avarice* of individuals of a nation that has coſt him ſo much of his *treaſure* and his *blood?* This is an inſult upon *common ſenſe*, as well as an unprecedented attack on *common juſtice!*

Had even the treaty of 1762 extended to the ſon of *Pertaub Sing* (which, it has been already proved it could not) that *ſon* ſhewed that he was not worthy of deriving any benefit from it. He manifeſted, upon every occaſion, a determined, an inveterate enmity to the *Engliſh* nation. He held an *avowed* correſpondence with their *avowed* enemies. He withheld his tribute from his *feudal ſuperior*, the Nabob of Arcot; and he added *inſult* to *diſobedience*. When he was required, by the Preſidency of Madras, to abſtain from *injuſtice*, he prepared for war. This induced the Preſidency to recur to the *poſitive orders* of the Court of Directors, relative to *Tanjore*.

Orders were accordingly iſſued to General Smith to lay ſiege to Tanjore. The place was inveſted in September 1771; but the Nabob, with more *hu-*

* The Company, as guarantees of the treaty, engaged "to the utmoſt of their power to "aſſiſt the party performing againſt the party failing to perform." Vide p. 117 of this Collection.

† Vide a letter under the ſeal of Governor Pigot, to the Killidars, Halmildars, &c. printed in the Appendix to *the State of Facts relative to Tanjore*.

manity than *policy*, accepted the *pretended* ſubmiſſion of the Zemindar, on the 24th of October. The rear of the army had ſcarce ceaſed to be ſeen, from the walls of Tanjore, when the *perfidious* Zemindar began to encourage the *Marattoes* to invade the Carnatic. The *Marattoes* accordingly, under the command of Trimbuckrow, entered the Carnatic, and pillaged the country; and the *Nabob* was obliged to ſave his dominions, by *buying off* thoſe plunderers. The intercepted letters of the Zemindar of Tanjore prove, beyond contradiction, that the invaſion was undertaken by his advice and at his inſtigation, at the very time he pretended to throw himſelf at the feet of the *Engliſh* and the *Nabob*, for forgiveneſs and mercy. When the *Marattoes* retreated, he renewed his applications for a *ſecond invaſion* of our territories; yet this *perfidious Zemindar* or *Renter* is the INJURED KING, whom *Lord Pigot* has reſtored to dominions which *never* belonged of *right* either to him or his family!

The intrigues of Tuljagee were not confined to the *Marattoes*. He ſent ſeveral embaſſies to *Hyder Ali*, the determined enemy of the *Engliſh*. He entered into the ſtricteſt connections with the *French*, the *Dutch*, and the *Danes*. With the *French* he actually concluded a treaty. Large ſums of money, an *excluſive* privilege of trade and valuable territories, were to have been exchanged for a body of Europeans and a train of artillery. He *ſold* whole diſtricts to the Dutch; he *mortgaged* others to the Danes. The *three* nations were to lend him their troops, to declare themſelves his allies, in his meditated war againſt the *Engliſh* and the Nabob: yet this is the *injured King*, whom Lord Pigot reſtores to dominions which *never* belonged to his family *!

When this ſtorm was gathering, the *Nabob* applied for the aid of the *Engliſh* to diſpoſſeſs a *perfidious Renter*, whom no treaties, no oaths could bind. The laws of *ſelf-preſervation*, as well as the laws of India, had rendered the meaſure indiſpenſably neceſſary. The matter was debated with a coolneſs ſuitable to its importance. The *pretended guarantee* of 1762 was carefully canvaſſed and ſcrupulouſly weighed. There was not a ſingle perſon at the Board ſo biaſſed in his judgment, ſo loſt to every idea of common juſtice, as to ſuppoſe, that a treaty *forced* by the *heavy hand* of power upon

* The intercepted letters, and papers proving all the facts mentioned in this paragraph, are printed in the Appendix to the *State of Facts relative to Tanjore.*

the

oo

the *Nabob*, had not expired with *Pertaub Sing*; even if it had not been broken, in *every article*, by his son, the *perfidious* Tuljagee †.

The necessity of displacing that Zemindar appeared to the whole Board. An expedition was resolved upon *unanimously*, as the only means to preserve the power of *this nation* on the coast. Sir Robert Harland, his Majesty's plenipotentiary in the Carnatic, urged, in the name of the King, the propriety of depriving Tuljagee of his Zemindary. His Majesty himself, in a letter dated in April 1772, had congratulated the *Nabob* upon the expedition in the year 1771. The *King of Great Britain*, in this letter *subscribed* by himself, is pleased to say, "It gave us satisfaction to hear, that the Go-" vernor and Council of Madras had sent the Company's troops with yours "to *reduce* your *tributary*, the *Raja of Tanjore*, to obedience; in which we "hope, with the *blessing of God*, they will be successful." The *King of Great Britain* calls the *Raja of Tanjore* a TRIBUTARY; yet *Lord Pigot* dignifies that very Raja with the title of *King*, and *restores* him to dominions which *never* belonged in property to his family!

It is now time to introduce *his Lordship's* KING to the acquaintance of the reader. When *Tuljagee* succeeded his father *Pertaub Sing*, as *Renter* of *Tanjore*, the first act of his government was expressive of the futility of his character and principles. He disgraced the servants of his father, and raised to the office of Minister, and to the command of his troops, a fellow whose former employment was to hold to him the *spitting-box*, when he chewed beetle-nut. He had been also his *Barawar* or *pimp*, which *honourable* office he continued to hold with that of Minister. In the capacity of *Barawar*, he recommended his *own sister* to Tuljagee; whilst, in that of *Minister*, he executed his most cruel and wanton orders. Tyranny, cruelty, oppression, laid waste the country without; riot, debauchery, and every species of vice, reigned within the palace. To supply the extravagance of the *Zemindar* and his *principal servant*, money was extorted from the wretched farmers by unheard-of tortures, and the cry of the oppressed people ascended to Heaven. There was, in short, no species of *public injustice*, none of *private profligacy*, which *Tuljagee* did not practise *himself* or encourage in *others*. The effects of drunkenness, riot, and debauchery, together with *disorders*

† The subject of the Treaty 1762, is discussed in the OBSERVATIONS annexed to these Papers.

incident to his courſe of pleaſures, enervated his mind and enfeebled his body. He often lay wallowing for whole days in the moſt beaſtly intoxication; and having, at times, acquired *fictitious* courage from the fumes of ſtrong liquors, he would talk of nothing but *extirpating the Engliſh*, or driving them out of India. But when danger came, he betrayed every ſymptom of terror; and his puſillanimity during the ſiege deprived him of that pity which is ſeldom denied to the unfortunate.

Such is the character of the profligate Zemindar, whom the India Company have raiſed to a *throne*, and the title of *King!* Neither his *Barawar Gilbilliapaw*, nor any one of the *Directors* who *ſigned* the orders for reſtoring him to his *pretended* dominions, can, with truth, affirm that the colouring is overcharged. The picture would be ſtill more like the *original*, had not his *ſecret* vices been left in the ſhade; but over theſe we ſhall draw a veil, for the honour of human nature. Such is the man for whom an *old* and *faithful* ally of *Great Britain* is *diſhonoured* and *ſtript* of his dominions, by ſome of the *ſubjects* of Great Britain, in direct *violation* of a *public treaty*, by which HIS MAJESTY guaranteed thoſe very dominions to the *Nabob* of *Arcot*. But it ſeems *Lord Pigot* guaranteed *Tanjore* to *Pertaub Sing*, in the year 1762; and therefore the *guarantee* of the KING OF GREAT BRITAIN muſt yield to *that* of his Lordſhip!!!

Preparatory to the injuſtice of reſtoring *Tanjore* to the diſplaced *Renter*, injurious reports of the bad treatment he met with from the Nabob were induſtriouſly propagated. The enemies of *Mahommed Ali* thought it neceſſary to *ruin* his reputation before they *robbed* him of his dominions. Nothing, however, could be more unjuſt. Upon the taking of *Tanjore*, the fort and country came into the hands of the *Nabob*, as a forfeiture from a rebellious *vaſſal* to his feudal lord. The *Renter* remained in his *palace*. He was ſcarcely leſs at large than when he ſecluded himſelf from the world for the gratification of his own *ſecret* and *abominable* vices. He received a revenue ſuitable to his rank. His mother, his women, his relations, the *companions* of his vices, (for who could be the friends of Tuljagee?) remained with him; and all were maintained at the *Nabob*'s expence. His mother and he himſelf were thoroughly ſatisfied with their ſituation. In a letter to the Nabob, which is now publiſhed, *ſhe* ſays, "I want words to expreſs my gratitude. "Be pleaſed to continue your friendſhip; we ſhall rely henceforth on your "Highneſs for ſupport." Tuljagee himſelf, in another letter, ſays, "Your

"Highneſs

" Highneſs is more dear to me, in my eſteem, than the deceaſed Maha-
" raja, (his father, *Pertaub Sing)* for your Highneſs has manifeſted a greater
" degree of kindeſs for me than ever he did *."

Upon the whole, it may be affirmed, with truth, that the opinion of the *Select Committee*, on the 22d of June 1773, when they deliberated on the expedition againſt *Tanjore*, was juſt in every reſpect. They *unanimouſly* agreed, " that it was *dangerous*, in the preſent ſyſtem, to have ſuch a power " as the *Raja* of *Tanjore* in the heart of the *Carnatic*; and that it was expe- " dient, for the ſafety of the *Carnatic* and the *Company's poſſeſſions*, that the " Raja of Tanjore ſhould be reduced." The meaſure, in fact, was founded on the law and principle of ſelf-defence. It has already appeared, from the conſtitution of the empire of the *Moguls*, and the nature of the feudal ſyſtem in India, that the Zemindar of *Tanjore*, as a *vaſſal* of the Carnatic, held his country by certain *tenures*, which he had avowedly and repeatedly *broken* and *violated*. In conſequence of ſuch breach and violation, his *feudal Lord* was authoriſed by the law of nations and every principle of juſtice to diſpoſ- ſeſs him. But if the Nabob was authoriſed to diſpoſſeſs him, by what *law* or by what *juſtice* did the Court of Directors take upon them to ſend *orders* to reſtore him, in breach of a *ſolemn treaty* made by the KING, and approved of by the *Parliament* of Great Britain? Is it juſt, or even is it *prudent*, for a few Directors in Leadenhall-ſtreet to violate, with *their orders*, the *engagements* of the Nation?

This buſineſs requires farther explanation. In the treaty of Paris, the Crowns of Great Britain and France expreſsly *guaranteed* Mahommed Ali, Nabob of Arcot, in *all* his poſſeſſions; that is, in the *whole* of the Carnatic. Tanjore is not only a *dependent province*, and its Zemindar a *vaſſal*, but it is alſo in the very heart of the dominions of the *Nabob*. Tanjore, therefore, is expreſsly comprehended in the *guarantee*, as a *part* of the *Carnatic* †. The

* Tuljagee never paſſed his time more agreeably, than when he lived a *nominal* priſoner in his own palace. The walls, which ſurround the palace and pleaſure-gardens, are near a mile in circumference. There he paſſed his time, with his women, mother, relations and friends. The whole time was ſpent in feſtivity and joy, in piping, dancing, and one continued round of diverſions. An Engliſh gentleman (Mr. Salmon) at preſent in London, who held a reſpectable office at Tanjore, and lived in that place till the Raja was reſtored, is ready to vouch for all theſe circumſtances.

† The ſubject is very fully canvaſſed and explained in the *Obſervations* annexed to theſe Papers.

treaty was made by *one*, and approved of by the *three* Eſtates of Parliament; it is, therefore, binding on *all* the ſubjects of Great Britain. What right have ſubjects to cede dominions *guaranteed* by the treaties of the Sovereign? Would not Parliament, ſhould the Nabob petition them, examine into this *daring breach* made by *individuals*, on the public faith? What anſwer will the *then* LEADING DIRECTORS give, when called to the Bar of the Houſe, to the queſtion, "Have YOU brought about by YOUR *Influence*, have YOU "authoriſed by YOUR Signature, the ceſſion of a territory *guaranteed* by the "Crown and Parliament of Great Britain †?"

The orders given to *Lord Pigot* for the reſtoration of Tanjore to the *diſplaced Renter*, were evidently founded on *falſe* as well as *unjuſt* principles. They take it for granted, with an effrontery ſcarce excuſable in the moſt *ignorant* (not to uſe a more ſevere epithet), that *Tuljagee*, the ſon of a *Baſtard*, and of the *race of an Uſurper*, is the *hereditary Sovereign* and *lawful Proprietor* of *Tanjore*. But the very reverſe has been repeatedly proved to the Public, and ought to have been *always* known to men who decide on the fate of empires.

The *orders* are, to the laſt degree, *unjuſt*; becauſe it has been *proved*, that the *Nabob* had an *inherent right*, as Subadar of the Carnatic, to diſpoſſeſs his *vaſſal*, the *Renter of Tanjore*, when he failed to perform his feudal duties. But if the right is *inherent* in the *Nabob*, what title has the Eaſt-India Company to reſtore his feudatory without his conſent? Is not the territory his own? Has the Company any right, has it even any *pretence* of claim on his dominions? Have the ſervants of the Company, have the *Directors* who ſigned the orders, a right, not only to break every tie which ought to bind themſelves, but even the *treaties* and *guarantees* of their Sovereign, the King of Great Britain, approved by the two other Eſtates of Parliament?

Did not the Company's Governor and Council deliver over, under the moſt ſolemn engagements, ſtipulations, and conditions, the fort and country of *Tanjore*, to its lawful Sovereign the *Nabob*? Has that unfortunate and oppreſſed Prince broke any part of the treaty? Nay, has he not fulfilled his engagements with the utmoſt juſtice and honour? What then can juſtify

† The objections raiſed againſt Tanjore's being comprehended in the national guarantee of 1763, are examined and *refuted*, in the *Obſervations* cited in the preceding note.

the

the Company to make ſuch a flagrant breach on *their* ſide? Do theſe *men* think that they will be permitted to break the *treaties* of the nation, to gratify their *reſentments*, or to ſerve their *intereſts?* What retribution can they make to the Company, ſhould the *Nabob* recover, in a *court of law*, more than *two millions Sterling*, for his expences in reducing *Tanjore?* What amends can they make to *Great Britain*, for involving her, perhaps, in a war? What, if France, who has, as well as Great Britain, *guaranteed* his dominions to the Nabob, ſhould make the ſupport of that *guarantee* a pretence of war? Are a few victims to *public juſtice* a ſufficient recompence to *this nation* for the lives of *thouſands* and the expence of *millions?* Are theſe events either improbable or impoſſible? And what proſpect have we of friends in the Eaſt, after having made ſuch a flagrant breach on the Nabob's undoubted rights? Is the oppreſſing and ruining *old friends* the way to acquire *new allies?* The patience of this nation has been great, but the nation was deſignedly miſled.

Upon every principle of expedience and policy, as well as of juſtice, the orders deſerve to be *reprobated*, and ought to be reverſed. *Lord Pigot* and the Directors who procured the orders have deprived of a rich country a power, whoſe fidelity Great Britain has long tried, whoſe attachment ſhe has long experienced. They reſtore it to another, who has been uniformly *treacherous* and *hoſtile*. The *former* is, from early affection and inclination, our *friend*; the *latter*, from early prejudices and recent injuries, our *enemy*. The *one* has added the affection of his *father*, to his own regard for the *Engliſh intereſt*; the *other* has joined an hereditary averſion to us, to his own particular regard for the *French intereſt*. But ſhould the *Renter* of *Tanjore* throw off his *natural diſpoſition*, and wiſh to be *grateful*, will not common prudence teach him not to put any truſt in *Britiſh faith?* Can a *newly-acquired Ally* place any confidence in our treaties, after we have broken every *public* and *private* tie, which bound us to an *old* and *faithful friend*, after we have *ſeized*, when we pretended to reſtore, his country, after keeping him in a manner a priſoner, when we boaſt of raiſing him to a throne *?

On the ground of expedience, a thouſand arguments might be urged from reverſing immediately the *orders*. Tanjore is one of the moſt fertile and

* See the letter written, it is ſuppoſed, by Lord Pigot to himſelf, in the name of Tuljagee; it is printed in this Collection.

moſt opulent provinces in the Decan. When it remained in the hands of the *hoſtile Renter*, whom *Lord Pigot* patronizes, the *French*, *Dutch*, and *Danes*, were enabled to provide more conſiderable inveſtments in the ſouthern countries than the *Engliſh* Company. But ſhould the French poſſeſs themſelves of the province of Tanjore, (a circumſtance which will infallibly follow its being reſtored to the former *profligate Renter*) they will derive from it great reſources of war; a revenue, proviſions, coolies, beaſts of burden. They will alſo interſect the Carnatic, and ſo cut off the communication between the ſouthern provinces and *our* principal force. Trichinopoly, Madura, Tinnevelly, the countries of the Great and Little Marawar, muſt fall into the hands of *French*: beſides, they will have it in their power to ſtarve Madras, by ſtopping the importation of grain from Trimili Waſh and other ſea-ports of *Tanjore*.

Should *Tanjore* remain in the hands of the *Nabob*, with an *Engliſh* garriſon in the fort, it would be impoſſible for an European enemy to march ſix miles from the coaſt, for want of coolies and beaſts of burden. The inveſtments of the Company might be increaſed; the reſources of *Tanjore*, inſtead of ſtrengthening our enemies, would ſupply *ourſelves* in war; our territories, and conſequently our commerce, would extend from the Ganges to Cape Comorin; the ſea on one ſide, the weſtern mountains on the other, would form a double barrier for *our* protection; and the Nabob, by the addition made to his revenue, would be enabled to entertain a body of horſe, to ſecure the country from the predatory incurſions of the Marattoes. Theſe being incontrovertible facts, what excuſe had the *Directors* for gratifying *Lord Pigot*, at the expence of the Britiſh nation? Had they been of the Duke de Choiſeul's cabinet, in the year 1770, they could not forward, with a greater appearance of *zeal*, or with more *real ſucceſs*, the views of that ambitious miniſter on the coaſt of Coromandel, which exactly correſponded with the arrangements made by their orders. *His* object was to eſtabliſh a *force* in the heart of our territories, and they have actually done with a *ſtroke* of the *pen*, what France *meditated* to do by the *ſword*.

On the univerſally admitted principles of juſtice, on thoſe of equity and common law, on thoſe of the law of nature and nations, in point of expedience and policy, on the ſcore of public treaties and ſolemn engagements, the *orders* ought to be *reprobrated*, and muſt be *reverſed*. An expedition is undertaken, a conqueſt is completed by the *expreſs orders* of the Company,

pany, and under the *ſanction* of the ſtate. This expedition and this conqueſt were carried on and finiſhed at the *ſole* expence of the *Nabob*. The *particulars* of that expence have been already made public *. They amount to between *two* and *three* millions ſterling. Is not the *Nabob* (NOW he is diſpoſſeſſed of Tanjore) entitled by *equity*, and even by *law*, to have his expences refunded? Who then is to refund this great ſum? Is the Company to be encumbered with a debt of millions, becauſe *a few Directors* have choſen to gratify *Lord Pigot*'s RESENTMENT, or to forward his INTEREST? Or will they, in *mere friendſhip*, pay the debt out of their own private fortunes? But granting that the *Directors*, by *aſſuming* the name of the Eaſt-India Company, are immediately freed from ſuits at law, will the legiſlature of this kingdom ſuffer an ally to be *robbed*, and *public treaties* to be *broken*, with *impunity?* Will even the Proprietors of India Stock ſit down in tranquillity, under the loſs of a free-gift of 400,000 l. and the expence of a body of horſe, and three battalions of ſeapoys, *for ever?* Will they bear with patience the paying the expences of the Nabob, becauſe Lord Pigot, by intrigues at the India-Houſe, obtained orders ſubverſive of every principle of juſtice, and every rule of policy? The *Directors* have been truly generous to *Lord Pigot* and his friend, the *Renter* of *Tanjore!* They break treaties to *pleaſe* his *Lordſhip:* they reſtore provinces to a man, who has been uniformly an *enemy* to Great Britain!!!

Some profligate perſons have been very buſy in adding *defamation* to *injuſtice*. They charge the *unfortunate Nabob* with *ambition*, and a *deſign* of *independence*. Where have they gathered this idle tale, or how can they ſupport it? The moſt inveterate of his enemies cannot produce a ſingle inſtance of his ever having entertained a wiſh of being *independent*. But ſhould accumulated acts of *oppreſſion*, *rapacity*, *indignity*, and of public and private *injuſtice*, ſuggeſt hereafter ſuch a deſign to his almoſt diſtracted mind, how is it poſſible for him to execute it? Are not his forts garriſoned with *our* troops, his army commanded by our officers, his own perſon, his children, his family, his ſervants, under the very guns of Fort St. George †? This *infamous aſperſion* has been raiſed by ſome of the ſervants of the Company, becauſe the *Nabob* has appealed to the *juſtice* of the Nation from the *injuſtice* of the Company, as well as of individuals in its ſervice.

* Vide the Appendix to the *State of Facts* lately publiſhed.

† Yet Lord Pigot made a motion in the Council at Madras, that it ſhould be *recommended* to the Nabob to remove to Arcot. His Lordſhip loſt the queſtion, on a diviſion, by a majority of *ſeven* to *four*.

ORIGINAL

ORIGINAL PAPERS

RELATIVE TO

TANJORE.

LORD Pigot, having obtained † orders, from the Court of Directors, to restore the province of Tanjore to the displaced Zemindar, arrived at Madras in the beginning of December 1775. The first three weeks after his Lordship's arrival passed in a *pretended* harmony with the Nabob of Arcot. It was certainly *pretended*, on the side of Lord Pigot; but, on that of the Nabob, it was really *serious*. He gave his Lordship some *valuable marks* of his confidence and friendship, which shall be fully explained in another place. When the *Eastern* ceremony of presents was over, Lord Pigot resolved to explain the object of his mission in the following letter.

† Lord Pigot's great and avowed object, in going to India, was the restoration of Tanjore to the displaced Renter. The Chairman and Deputy-chairman of the Court of Directors, at the time, were no strangers to his Lordship's wishes on this head; yet it was only proposed, at first, to *intercede* with the Nabob, for an assignment of an allowance proper for the Raja, and a guard for the protection of his person. Lord Pigot, however, by his frequent visits to the India-House, OBTAINED, as mentioned in the text, the orders for the total restoration of Tanjore. This was a point of great difficulty, notwithstanding the utmost exertion of influence and intrigue. The orders lay a fortnight in the India-House, before a *legal* number of signatures could be obtained in the Court of Directors; and they were at last signed, on the very day of the *annual election*, the 17th of April 1775, when the Court of Proprietors were met to chuse *new* Directors, and consequently for the time, suspended the authority of the *old*.

Letter from Lord Pigot to the Nabob, dated 30th December, 1775.

To the Nabob.

May it pleaſe your Highneſs,

UNDERSTANDING from your ſons, Umdaht-ul-Omrah and Ameer-ul-Omrah, whom I had the honour to ſee this morning, that it was your wiſh, I ſhould communicate to you in writing the purport of the Orders I have received from the Company reſpecting Tanjore, I think I cannot comply with your requeſt in a more ſatisfactory manner, than by giving you an extract of thoſe orders.

" In order to remedy ſo far as may be the inconveniencies occaſioned by the miſconduct of our late Preſident and Council, we have thought proper to conſtitute, and by our commiſſion under our ſeal, dated the 11th inſtant, have conſtituted and appointed you, to be our Governor and Council of Fort St. George, for governing and managing all the Company's affairs on the coaſt of Coromandel and Orixa, and all our Forts, Factories, and Settlements thereunto belonging; ſubject however to the limitations and reſtrictions contained in a late Act of Parliament, intituled, ' An Act for ' eſtabliſhing certain regulations for the better management of the affairs ' of the Eaſt India Company, as well in India as in Europe.' It behoves you to avoid all meaſures of a like tendency with thoſe which have involved our ſervants in *the conſequences of our diſpleaſure* *.

" In the execution of the truſt now repoſed in you, ſeveral important objects claim your immediate and moſt ſerious conſideration. We ſhall point out what we wiſh to have accompliſhed, and ſuggeſt ſuch means as appear to us moſt likely to be effectual for obtaining the ends propoſed; but we are convinced that ſucceſs muſt in a great meaſure depend upon the wiſdom of your Councils, the integrity and firmneſs of your conduct, and in no ſmall degree upon the ſeaſonable exertion of thoſe peculiar abilities for which your right honourable Preſident is ſo juſtly and eminently diſtinguiſhed ‡.

* This expreſſion is highly ridiculous and abſurd; and totally *inconſiſtent* with the Orders of the Year 1769. It is ridiculous, becauſe the few Directors who ſigned the Orders aſſume the language of ſovereignty; and abſurd, becauſe it contradicts the expreſs Orders of a former Court.

‡ The world will be probably enabled to judge concerning the *juſtice* of this *eulogium,* after peruſing the following papers.

" As

"As the solemn promise made by our Governor and Council, at the request of the Nabob of the Carnatic and the King of Tanjore, to guarantee the Treaty of 1762, has been fully approved by the Court of Directors, we cannot but consider the public faith of the Company as forfeited, and the honour of the British nation deeply affected, by the measures taken for dethroning that unhappy prince, whose kingdom has been wrested from him by our servants, and put under the government of Mahommed Ali Cawn, in direct violation of that Treaty, and *contrary to our repeated orders and instructions, which have uniformly and expressly prohibited them from attempting to enlarge our own or the Nabob's dominions* ‡.

"And as we have resolved to contribute, so far as in us lies, towards the restoration of the king of Tanjore, which, by every tie of honour, we conceive ourselves bound to do, we hereby direct that you take the most effectual measures, without loss of time, for securing the person of the king of Tanjore; and that you forthwith appoint him a *proper guard for his protection, and also for the protection of his family* *; and inform him, that we have determined to replace him upon the *throne of his ancestors*, upon certain terms and conditions to be agreed upon for the mutual benefit of himself and the English East India Company, without *infringing the rights of Mahommed Aly Cawn, Nabob of the Carnatic* †.

"As

‡ The Directors who signed the Orders fall here into an absurdity. *General principles* can ONLY govern, where there are no *positive* or *specific orders*; a contrary position would be subversive of all government; and indeed is, in itself, so ridiculous and absurd, that it was never adopted by any state or society whatever. It remained for the Directors of the 12th of April 1775, to hold forth to the world this strange position," *Our servants have incurred* OUR *displeasure, for obeying our* POSITIVE ORDERS.

* The anxiety here expressed, by the Directors, for the protection of the person of Tuljagee, is superfluous. He was in perfect safety in his own palace, and scarce more confined, than when he sat (as it is here *intelligently* expressed) *on the throne of his ancestors*. The palace of Tanjore is very large, with gardens of pleasure so extensive, that the wall, which surrounds both, is little short of a mile in circumference. Here Tuljagee ranged at pleasure, with his family, women, relations and friends. Not a person belonging to the Nabob, lived within the gates; and those who were without, *acted entirely as his servants*. The palace was a perpetual scene of festivity and joy; dancing, piping, and every sign and demonstration of happiness. Women were brought to him from every corner of India, as when he sat on the Musnud; and, indeed, Tuljagee had the candour to own to Lord Pigot himself, that he never lived more happily than since his country fell into the hands of the Nabob.

† Ignorance cannot possibly be admitted as an excuse for the absurdity of this injunction. The

Directors

" As our faith stands pledged by the Treaty of 1762, to obtain payment of the King of Tanjore's tribute to the said Nabob of the Carnatic, as it is our interest and sincere desire to maintain the public tranquillity, and as we find, to our great concern, that other Europeans have obtained *undue influence in Tanjore*, which if permitted and encouraged may operate unfavourably for the Company, render it difficult to perform the part of guarantee to the said Treaty, and even tend to *endanger the peace of the country*; we therefore direct, that you declare to the King of Tanjore, that as we have no security for the performance of *any engagements* which may be entered into by him, and as in times past the payment of the tribute has been evaded or delayed, and several of his districts *mortgaged to Europeans*, contrary to the *interests of the Company* ‡, we shall insist upon his admitting a garrison of our troops into the Fort of Tanjore, not only to insure the regular payment of the Nabob's just demand in future, but also to enable us effectually to watch the motions, and to counteract the views, of any European or Country power, who may attempt to form connections, or make establishments, in Tanjore, to our prejudice; and you are likewise to insist upon having an assignment of revenues made to the Company, sufficient for the maintenance of the said troops, and for providing military stores necessary for the defence of the garrison.

" You are however, in our name, to assure the King of Tanjore, that no *diminution of his authority* over his subjects is intended by us, and that we

Directors desire Lord Pigot not to *infringe the rights of the Nabob*; yet they, with one dash of the pen, give away his dominions and conquests, obtained in a necessary and regular war.

‡ It appears, from this paragraph, that the authors of the Orders *deliberately*, and with their eyes open, do great injustice to an ally of Great Britain. They declare themselves no strangers to the hostile conduct of the Raja; they own, that other Europeans had obtained undue influence over his counsels; that this circumstance tended to endanger the peace of the country, and that they had no security for the performance of his engagements; that he had evaded the payment of the tribute, and had mortgaged several of his districts to Europeans. This and much more the Raja did; yet *they restore* him to power, and throw into his hands the means of working the destruction of the Company. By what rule or line of policy can this be accounted for? How can men, entrusted by their constituents to manage their affairs, thus deliberately destroy the interest they were meant to protect? By their misconduct, they have endangered the valuable trade and great resources of this country on the coast; and have thus given a fatal stab to the Company. One might be tempted to ask, are such men fit to dispose of kingdoms, and to govern empires; or is it prudent in the State, to suffer the great interest of the nation to be sacrificed to influence, or lost by ignorance.

will

will ſeverely puniſh every military officer, or Company's ſervant, who ſhall in any reſpect interfere in the affairs of his government; and you are to take eſpecial care that this article be punctually fulfilled on the part of the Company.

" Although juſtice to our own honour, and to the King of Tanjore, compels us to take meaſures for delivering him out of the hands of the Nabob of the Carnatic, you are neverthelcſs to declare publicly, in our name, that we will by no means protect the King of Tanjore in with-holding from Mahommed Aly Cawn his ſtipulated tribute of four lacks of rupees *per annum*, or any part of it; but that on the contrary we will do our utmoſt to procure payment thereof to the ſaid Nabob.

" We direct, that in caſe the King of Tanjore ſhall not be living at the time of your receipt hereof at Fort St. George, you forthwith proceed to place the next of the royal line, or ſome other proper perſon of the King of Tanjore's family, upon the throne of his anceſtors, ſubject however to all terms and conditions required by the Company, reſpecting Tanjore, in theſe our orders and inſtructions *.

" If any of our ſervants, civil or military, ſhall oppoſe the execution of theſe our orders and inſtructions, or refuſe to aſſiſt in carrying them into full effect, we hereby declare, that upon proper repreſentation of the caſe to us, every ſuch perſon ſhall be abſolutely diſmiſſed from the ſervice of the Company.

" And in order to add the greateſt weight in our power to our proceedings, and to inſure, as far as may be, ſucceſs to your meaſures, we have directed our Governor-general and Council of Bengal to co-operate with you, if you ſhall find it neceſſary, and to yield you all proper aſſiſtance in bring-

* Upon this paragraph ſeveral remarks might be made. There is " more than meets the " ear meant;" by theſe words, " in caſe the King of Tanjore ſhall not be living." To facilitate the Orders, reports were propagated, " that the Raja's life was in danger."—This was a falſehood. He was ſaid to have been " removed to Trichinopoly:"—This was alſo an impudent fiction. Men, who ought to be (and actually were) better informed, ſaid, he was " kept a cloſe pri-" ſoner;"—this was a purpoſely fabricated calumny. He is here called a *king*, yet he is the great-grandſon of a Maratto Freebooter, who, by a piece of unheard-of treachery, ſeized Tanjore, when he was called to defend it.

ing

ing the important affairs hereby committed to your management to a ſpeedy and happy concluſion †.

I have the honour to be
Your Highneſs's moſt obliged,
and obedient humble ſervant,

Fort St. George,
30th December, 1775.

PIGOT."

The Orders contained in the preceding letter have been already expoſed as unjuſt, inexpedient, and impolitic, in the *State of Facts*, now in the hands of the Public. The *Raja* of Tanjore is ignorantly called *King* of that place, though it is known that his anceſtors were originally uſurpers and always vaſſals. It is the cuſtom of illiterate and ill-informed perſons in both the Indies, to call Chiefs, by the name of Kings. The negro in Madagaſcar who proſtitutes his daughter for a glaſs of arrack to the Midſhipman of an Eaſt India-man; and the ſavage Cherokee, who ſells a bearſkin to the North American trader for half a blanket, are dignified with *royal titles.* Thus we hear of the *ſtanding turkey* KING, on the confines of Virginia; and thus, of the kings of Johanna and Tanjore.

Upon the ground of expedience, a thouſand arguments might be produced, againſt the meaſure of reſtoring Tanjore to the Raja. That province is one of the moſt fertile and opulent countries in the Decan. When it remained in the hands of the Raja, the Dutch, as well as the French and Danes, were enabled to provide more conſiderable inveſtments in the ſouthern countries, than the Engliſh Company. But, ſhould the French poſſeſs themſelves of the country (a circumſtance ſcarce to be doubted, ſhould it happen to be reſtored to the Raja), they will derive from it great reſources for war, and be enabled to interſect the Nabob's dominions, and ſo cut off the communication between the ſouthern provinces and our principal force in the Carnatic. Trichinopoly, Madura, Tinnevelly, the countries of the great and little Marawar, would, in ſuch caſe, inevitably fall into their hands; beſides, they would have it in their power to ſtarve Madras, by ſtopping the exportation of grain, from Trimili Waſh, and other ſea-ports of Tanjore *.

† There is a *vehement ſincerity* in theſe Orders, a ſtrength of *wiſh*, if not of *expreſſion*, which ſhews, that the labourer is worthy of his hire; only *one perſon* is meant, *et verbum ſat ſapienti.* We may ſay to the *reſt*, in the language of holy writ, "they *knew* not what they did."

* Should Tanjore remain in the hands of the Nabob, it would be impoſſible for any European enemy to march ſix miles from the coaſt, for want of coolies and beaſts of burden.

On

On the other hand, ſhould the country remain in the poſſeſſion of the Nabob, the inveſtments of the Company might be increaſed; the reſources of Tanjore, inſtead of ſtrengthening the enemies of the Nabob, would provide the means of aiding his friends with ſucceſs; our territory, and conſequently our commerce, would extend from the Ganges to Cape Comorin; the ſea on the one ſide, the weſtern mountains on the other, would form a double barrier for our protection; and the Nabob, by the addition made to his revenue, would be able to entertain a body of horſe, to ſecure the country from the depredatory incurſions of the Marattoes.

The orders given to Lord Pigot, for the reſtoration of Tuljagee, were in every light founded on falſe as well as unjuſt principles. They take it for granted, that Tuljagee is the hereditary ſovereign and proprietor of Tanjore. But it is demonſtrable, that his firſt anceſtor was an uſurper, and the whole line vaſſals. Pertaub Sing, the father of the preſent Raja, a baſtard of the line of the firſt uſurper, was himſelf, in conſequence of his miſdemeanors, as a vaſſal of the empire, depoſed and confined by his feudal lord, the Nabob of the Carnatic. During his confinement he received only half a crown a day for his ſubſiſtence; and few, who knew the character of the man, thought the allowance too ſmall.

The orders are unjuſt, becauſe the Nabob had an inherent right in himſelf, as Subahdar of the Carnatic, to diſpoſſeſs his vaſſal, the Zemindar of Tanjore, when he failed in his obedience. But, if the Nabob's right of diſpoſſeſſing is inherent in his office, what right has the Company to reſtore his feudatory, without his conſent? Is not the territory his own? Have we any right or claim to his dominions? Should it even be allowed, that the Company, or rather a few Directors, may with impunity encroach on the authority of Mahommed Ali, have they a right to break through every tie that binds ſtates and corporate bodies? Did not their Governor and Council, in the moſt ſolemn manner, deliver over to the Nabob, the fort and country of Tanjore, on certain ſtipulations and conditions? Has the Nabob broke any part of the treaty, to juſtify a breach on the Company's ſide? Has not the government of this kingdom, in the perſon of the King's repreſentative, given its ſanction, to the conqueſt? And does the Company preſume to abrogate the deed of the nation?

 The

The orders are incompatible with every idea of juſtice, on other grounds. An expedition is undertaken, and a conqueſt completed, with the aid and ſanction of the Company and of the State. This expedition, and this conqueſt, were carried on and finiſhed, at the ſole expence of the Nabob. That expence was enormous: Prize money to the army, donations to the principal ſervants, a voluntary gift of 400,000*l.* to the Company, a ſum nearly equal to redeem, from the Dutch and Danes, the diſtricts, which Tuljagee had either *mortgaged* or *ſold* to thoſe nations; together with immenſe ſums laid out in improving the country, in ſupplying with ſeed and bullocks the farmers, impoveriſhed by the rapacious cruelty of Tuljagee, and on the fortifications of Tanjore, by the expreſs advice of the preſidency, and under the inſpection of one of the Company's Engineers ‡.

But, if the Company chuſe to be unjuſt to the Nabob, is it conſiſtent with common prudence, to be unjuſt to themſelves? If the Nabob muſt be diſpoſſeſſed of Tanjore, has he not an undoubted claim in equity, if not in law, to have the ſums he has expended on the conqueſt, refunded? Is it a trifling conſideration to the proprietors, to loſe the free gift of 400,000 *l.* Is it a matter of no conſequence to be deprived of the pay of three battalions of Sepoys, from the year 1769, to the reſtoration of Tanjore, in terms of the Treaty? Did not the Nabob agree to maintain ten inſtead of ſeven battalions; and did he not engage to raiſe a body of horſe, ſo neceſſary for the defence of our poſſeſſions? The Company have truly carried their generoſity to Tuljagee, their avowed enemy, to a pitch beyond example. They not only break treaties, but either forego or ſquander treaſures, to gratify a profligate young man, who will uſe his good fortune, only as the means of purſuing with more eaſe his own abominable vices.

‡ Nothing could equal the diſtreſs of the country during the government of Tuljagee. No man's property was ſafe, no woman's chaſtity ſecure. The wretched inhabitants, reduced to poverty by his unheard-of extortions, *ſold* their children for a rupee a head. The French and Dutch, availing themſelves of that circumſtance, carried this ſpecies of commerce to ſuch a height, that the Nabob, after he had taken poſſeſſion of the country, was obliged to put a ſtop to the *exportation* of children by an edict; and to alleviate the diſtreſſes, which had forced parents to become the ſellers of their own offſpring, that humane prince placed a number of perſons, in every diſtrict, to boil and diſtribute rice to the poor. Theſe are facts of public notoriety; and ſtand in need of no proofs.

The

The orders are as contrary to true policy, as they are destitute of common justice. We deprive a power, whose fidelity we have long tried, whose attachment we have long experienced, of a rich country. We restore it to another, who has been uniformly treacherous and hostile. The former is, from habit and inclination, our friend. The latter from early prejudices, as well as on account of recent injuries, our enemy. The one has added the affection of his father, to his own regard, for the English interest; the other has joined an hereditary aversion to his own particular resentment. But granting that the Raja may wish to be grateful to the Company, will not common prudence teach him to put no trust in British faith? Can a newly acquired ally place any confidence in our treaties, after we have broken all the public and private ties which bound us to an old and faithful friend?

Men who wish to cover injustice with an excuse of expediency, have charged the Nabob with ambition, and a design of emancipating himself from the controul of the Company. The injustice of the Company has not been able to suggest a wish of that kind to his injured mind. But he may defy the most inveterate of his enemies to produce a single instance of such a wish. But should he entertain any design of that kind, how is it possible for him to execute it? Are not his forts garrisoned with our troops? His army commanded by our officers? Is not his country open to our invasion? His person always in our power? Is not he himself, are not his children, his family, his servants, under the very guns of fort St. George? This silly calumny of independence has been fabricated by some of the Company's servants, who were jealous of the Nabob's correspondence with Government. But had he met with justice from the Company, he would not now stand in need of the protection of the sovereign, and the justice of the nation, for securing his rights and establishing his authority.

To shew the injustice of insinuating in the orders, that the Raja's person was in danger, the following letter from the Nabob's military governor at Tanjore is submitted to the reader.

Tranſlation of a Letter from Mahomed Nagif Cawn, dated 1ſt Jummaudalouwell 1189 Hegira, received on the 4th.

I Have received the favour of your Highneſs's gracious letter dated the 29th Rabbaſauney, wherein your Highneſs is pleaſed to mention, that your enemies report that the Raja Tuljagee and his wife killed themſelves; and that I ſhould particularly inform your Highneſs of the preſent ſituation of the Raja, and all his family.

I am aſtoniſhed at what your Highneſs mentions. This ſtory was made by people who wanted ſomething to talk about, and diſturbers who invent lies; no ſuch thing has happened in the Raja's family ſince the reduction of Tanjore, to give riſe to any ſuch report as diſturbers have propagated: however, by the bleſſing of God and your Highneſs's favour, the Raja, his mother, his father's other widow, his own two wives, his younger brother, his *daughter and his ſon* †, are all in good health and ſpirits, beſides his relations ſlaves both men and women, and his attendants, who are in houſe, are all very well. Of all the people who have been from the beginning in the Raja's houſe, there has but one died, who was a relation and above eighty years old; he was carried off four or five months ago, by a tedious ſickneſs. This I informed your Highneſs of at the time it happened; all the other people are in good health and ſpirits, and Tuljagee often expreſſes his thanks to your Highneſs, and his ſatisfaction in his manner of living. The Circar people who are at his gates, act entirely as his ſervants, except in taking care of the gates according to my order.

Lord Pigot had arrived in the beginning of December; and received a ſervice of gold plate, horſes, carriages, and other preſents, from the Nabob. Finding *nothing more could be done* at Madras, he bethought himſelf of the Company's orders, and reſolved to make a journey to Tanjore. Yet, as things were not *ſufficiently prepared* for his reception at Tanjore, he did not ſet out for that place till the beginning of April. The intermediate time, from December 1775 till April 1776, being *four months*, he employed in conferences and correſpondences with the Nabob.

† By concubines.

Translation of a Conference between his Highness the Nabob and Lord Pigot.

ON the 19th Zucaud 1189 Hegiry, or 12th January 1776, his Lordship came to his Highness, and told him, that he could not express to his Highness how much his (his Lordship) honour was hurt by the delay in his business, and that he would wait on his Highness to-morrow morning, to ask a single question from him, and was then going to take his leave, and went away.—His Lordship stood for some time in the Nabob's garden with Omdaht-ul-Omrah, Ameer-ul-Omrah, and Syful Mulk Behawders, and told them, that he never suffered so much disgrace in his whole life; that he was a *man of family*, and had *friends* and *money*; that it was not necessary to him to return to this country, and to take so much business on himself, with any view of advantage to himself, but that he came here in friendship to the Nabob; that the Nabob would not yet give him up the Fort of Tanjore, but that he would ask him to-morrow morning, whether he, his Lordship, must go to Tanjore in order to place an English garrison there, or should send Sir Robert Fletcher, or any other councellor, that his Highness might approve of. His Lordship further said, that the business of the country was but trifling and might be settled afterwards; and that he would never set his name to a letter to the Company, till he could mention that this business was settled; but that the Council might write that he was gone to Tanjore for that purpose. That he would to-morrow morring go into his Pallenkeen, and set off for Tanjore, and there declare, that the same troops belonging to his Masters, who took the Fort of Tanjore and delivered it to the Nabob, now want the possession of the Fort again; and that he would see whether the Nabob's troops would fire on him or not; that he hoped to God that the day would never come, when he should be obliged to send for the Company's troops from the seaports and the Circars, to take the Fort by force; that this business must be settled before the departure of the Europe ship; and that he would sooner be *hanged* or have his head *cut off*, than give up his honour. Seyful Mulk on hearing this expression turned so pale, that his Lordship expressed words of comfort to him.

The harſh treatment received by the Nabob, from Lord Pigot, in the preceding conference, had thrown the unfortunate prince into a ſevere illneſs. His ſons were, therefore, appointed to confer with his Lordſhip.

Tranſlation of a conference between Omdaht-ul-Omrah, Ameer-ul-Omrah Behawders, and Lord Pigot, 24th Zucaud 1189 Hegiry, or 16th January 1776.

OMDAHT-UL-OMRAH, and Ameer-ul-Omrah went this morning to Lord Pigot, who was waiting at his garden gate to receive them; when he ſaw them, he advanced towards them crying. They were ſurpriſed, and enquired after his health; he told them, that he did not ſleep a moment laſt night, becauſe buſineſs goes on worſe and worſe, and that his arguments were of no conſequence; that the Nabob was become an enemy to the Company, and that the friendſhip between him and his Lordſhip was broken from this day. They aſked him how he could ſay ſo, that his Highneſs would give up his life, fortune, family, and all his countries to the Company, but would by no means become their enemy. His Lordſhip ſaid, that the Nabob would not comply with the Company's order. They obſerved, that the arguments between his Lordſhip and his Highneſs had been upon buſineſs, and as his Lordſhip had expreſſed his ſentiments, it was proper his Highneſs ſhould do the ſame, therefore his Lordſhip ſhould not ſay that his Highneſs was become an enemy to the Company. Lord Pigot ſaid, the Company do not wiſh to have all the countries, but only wiſh to ſettle this buſineſs. They then went into the garden houſe, where his Lordſhip cried very much, and would not ſpeak or ſit down for an hour, and could not ſhew his face. His Lordſhip produced a paper, a copy of which he ſent to his Highneſs by Omdaht-ul-Omrah, that his Highneſs might copy it, and ſend it to him. His Lordſhip read it and cried, and they comforted him and put their hands on his feet, deſiring (for God's ſake) that his Lordſhip would be ſo good as to put off this buſineſs till he received further orders from England, and that in the mean time he might put an Engliſh garriſon in Tanjore, and that his Highneſs would increaſe the Raja's allowances, and when he ſhould be more fully convinced of the determination of the Company and his Lordſhip, he would comply with them. That enforcing this buſineſs with his Highneſs, was as bad to him

as

as cutting his throat! Lord Pigot said he could not wait, and that his crying was for this, that after he should be obliged to settle this business by force, how could he look in the face of his old father, meaning his Highness, and that this was the last day he would come to the garden, but would stay in the fort; that he would remain all this day at the garden, and would not even go to his dinner. He frequently said, that he had ruined himself; he exclaimed, why did he come upon this business? That if he had not come upon this business, the fall of the house would not have happened: That when this business was finished he was sure the Nabob would not survive it: That the sin and great trouble would be upon him. Why did he come here? If he had not made a proper peace between the Nabob and the Raja, he would not have been brought into this trouble; but that some rascals had, since his departure for Europe, broke that peace. Omdaht-ul Omrah and Ameer-ul Omrah then came away.

In about an hour after, they returned to his Lordship; he said then, that he was a little better; that when his mind was overwhelmed wirh sorrow, he found relief in shedding tears; that he would now converse: That there were several rascals and disturbers about the Nabob who gave him bad advice: That the Nabob should (through his favour to him) never listen to their advice: That he had not stopped any gentleman from going to the Nabob, but had told him, that whoever he thought proper might go to him, and give him advice: That he had done so, that his Highness might be assured, that he (his Lordship) was firmly determined in this business, and that he might see that it was so: That it would be better if his Highness did not listen to their advice, and that if he would permit him, he would prevent their going to him: His Lordship further said, if this business should be carried into execution by disagreeable measures, it would not be then in his power to shew any friendship to the Nabob: That people would say, where was the advantage of sending Lord Pigot on this business? Any man might do it by force, then what extraordinary good has Lord Pigot done? If the Company and the Nabob keep up such a large body of troops, what will be the consequence? They cannot pay them, therefore 'tis proper that they should reduce them, and regulate their business. They will then attend to their affairs, and they should establish a treasury; they will then be ready

ready to undertake any thing that may be neceſſary ; there will be no harm if matters ſhould not be conducted to the Nabob's ſatisfaction for two years, as after that time his affairs would be in a good ſituation. His Lordſhip further ſaid, that he was not acquainted with Mr. Haſtings, though he had been twice in his company at Mr. Vanſittart's houſe, and once in his company in England; that he had heard he had ſeveral ſuch raſcals about him as Mr. Stewart, who is here now, and that he liſtened to their advice: That General Clavering was a very good and honeſt man, and though General Monſon was an enemy to the Company, he was a brave officer, and a man of ſenſe : That he (his Lordſhip) did not know in what manner buſineſs would be ſettled in England, and that his Highneſs ſhould not place any confidence in raſcals, or give any money to them, as it could be of no ſervice to him. Omdaht-ul-Omrah and Ameer-ul-Omrah told his Lordſhip, that on ſeeing his weeping and affliction, they had gone to his Highneſs, but could not ſee him as he was ill ; that they had heard that his Highneſs was laid down, therefore they would ſit down and converſe with his Lordſhip, and would this evening or to-morrow morning again ſee him in the Company's garden. His Lordſhip replied, perhaps he might not have time to-morrow morning, as he would be employed at the Seſſions; they ſaid, they would then ſee him the day after to-morrow; but his Lordſhip ſaid, he would come to-morrow morning to the garden. They then took their leave, and his Lordſhip ſent his reſpectful compliments to his Highneſs.

The Nabob being a little recovered from his illneſs, wrote the following letter to Lord Pigot; hoping, perhaps, from the profuſion of his Lordſhip's *tears*, at the conference of the 16th, that he would *relent*, and liſten to his propoſals, as well as have *ſome* regard to his *rights*. The letter is an anſwer to that of his Lordſhip of December 30 1775.

Tranſlation of a Letter from his Highneſs the Nabob, to the Right Honourable George Lord Pigot, &c. &c. dated 29th Zecaud, or 22d January, 1776.

I Have received your Lordſhip's letter, containing an extract of the Company's order to you relative to Tanjore. I am convinced that the Gentlemen of the Company were *entirely unacquainted* with the ſituation of affairs here,

here *, and with the true reaſons for taking Tanjore, as alſo with my rights, when they wrote ſuch orders as they now have, and have been influenced by falſe and groundleſs reports, or they would not have given them.

I underſtand that it has been repreſented to the people of England, that I have taken Tanjore through ambitious motives, and that I and my ſon treated in an oppreſſive manner Tuljagee and his family †. As you are a well-wiſher to the Company, and my old friend, and are come here on their part, I beg that your Lordſhip will make ſtrict inquiry into the truth of ſuch reports as prevailed in England. As the Gentlemen of the Company are not acquainted with the true ſtate of affairs, it is neceſſary that I ſhould mention ſome things for their information.

Being ſenſible of the bad conduct of Tuljagee, his connections with the French, Dutch, Danes, Hyder, and other Powers, his ſelling and mortgaging ſome diſtricts of the Tanjore country to other Europeans than the Engliſh, and receiving aſſiſtance from them in troops, military ſtores, &c. his ſending large ſums of money, and an Ambaſſador to the Marratta Chiefs, to induce them to bring their troops to make diſturbances in the Carnatic and to deſtroy the country; his making uſe of perſuaſions with other Powers to engage them in the ſame meaſures; his having aſſiſted Hyder with money, proviſions and other things which he ſtood in need of, in his invaſion of the Carnatic; his making an expedition againſt the Marawars and Mallacotty, which are my tributaries, and taking from them great ſums of money, jewels, horſes, elephants, guns, &c. though the Governor and Council and I forbid him this proceeding; and his not paying him tribute, which the Company obſerved in their orders he had delayed. In order to ſecure the tranquillity of the Carnatic, I thoughtit neceſſary to explain the matters full to your former Governors.

* This is the moſt favourable conſtruction he could put upon the abſurd Orders of the Court of Directors; if indeed they were a *Court* when they ſigned them. This is a matter which a court of *law* can only decide. They were certainly not *entirely unacquainted* with the ſituation of the Carnatic. The reader is requeſted to look back to page 4, where this ſubject is fully diſcuſſed.

† Theſe miſrepreſentations are now removed by facts.

From

From the beginning of my connection with the Company, my business has been conducted (as it is at present) by the approbation of the Governor and Council, and I have always considered the Governor and Council as the Company. Governor Du Pré himself, who was deputy to Tanjore in the year 1762, to make a peace and settle matters; who afterwards went to England, was appointed a Director there, and came here as Governor of Fort St. George, was well acquainted with the sentiments of the Company. He as well as the Gentlemen of the Company (as appears by their letter to me, dated the 17th March 1769, mentioning their trust and confidence in the wisdom of Mr. Du Pré, whose conduct was approved by them on his return to England) thought the behaviour of Tuljagee in the year 1771, contrary to the treaty made in 1762, and to the interests and honour of the Company and me; and subversive of the peace and tranquillity of the Carnatic, and the Company's possessions and commerce; and employed their troops (by the advice of Governor-general Hastings, who was then second in Council at Fort St. George, and the other Counsellors and the King's Ministers) with mine to take the fort and country of Tanjore; and to put them into my hands. In Mr. Du Pré's letter, dated the 15th Jemaudesanny 1185 Hegira, or 25th September 1771, he acquainted me with the Company's order for giving me assistance. A copy of our correspondence on this subject has been sent to the Court of Directors. At that time Tuljagee submitted to me, and agreed to discharge the tribute, and act in a different manner from what he had formerly done. For the performance of which, he gave an obligation under his seal; and in consequence I recalled my troops from that country, though I might then have got possession of the fort of Tanjore, and it was then the real wish of the Governor and Council that I should do so; but he did not attend many days to his promises and submission, but resumed his former bad conduct. On the return of the Company's and my troops to Trichinopoly, when peace was concluded on the 17th Rajeb 1185 Hegira, he prevailed on Trimuckrow (who was at that time in the command of forty thousand horse in the Hyder's country) by giving him large sums of money, to send twenty thousand of them to his assistance; in consequence whereof, on the 5th Shawban Trimuckrow crossed the Gauts, and his troops plundered my country as far as Callespawk, but I prevailed on them to retire, on giving them a great deal of money; besides this, Tuljagee applied to the Dutch for their assistance, and they gave it it in the strongest manner, as may appear by the letter of the Governor General of Batavia to me, dated the 26th July 1771, regarding his giving assistance to Tuljagee. Tuljagee's bad conduct I have mentioned to your late governor Mr. Wynch, in my letter of the 18th of June 1773, or 26th Rabbelowell 1187 Hegira. He, General Smith, and all the Council thought it very proper and necessary, to take possession of his country, and sent the Company's troops with mine a second time against him; and by the blessing of God, the Fort and country fell into my hands; but I continued Tuljagee and all his family in his Palace in the Fort, and ordered honour and respect to be observed to them as before; there is not the least alteration in his table, nor amongst his family. It is due to the reduction of this place, that all interior disturbances in my country (recommended to my attention by the Company's letter of the 4th of March 1767) are at an end, according to their wishes. Had it not been for the capture of Tanjore, we cannot say what troubles might not have since prevailed in the country, because Tanjore is so situated in the middle of my country, that it cannot be attacked by an enemy, without their first passing through my country. It is now five years since Governor Du Pré gave orders to take the Fort of Tanjore, and employed the Company's troops for that purpose; and it is near three years that Tanjore has been taken, as has been already known to the Company at home; *but they have been silent on the subject* *. I have paid large sums of money to the Europeans of other nations, which they demanded from Tuljagee, for the release of some districts which he had sold to them; besides, I paid considerable sums which he owed to individuals, and to his army, as also the expence of the Company's army and mine; and I have prevented the Marrattas from coming into this country, by buying them off with a large sum of money.

I have borrowed considerable sums from English gentlemen, who lent them to promote the capture of Tanjore. I have, besides, borrowed from the people of the country large sums of money, which I expended in improving it, in repairing the water-courses, the mounds, and the fortifications, which last was done by Major Stephens, a Company's engineer. I have made great advances to the inhabitants, towards buying bullocks and seed

* This silence certainly implied the entire approbation of the measure.

grain;

grain; and I have borrowed Paddy ſeed from the country people, &c. and given it to the inhabitants, which has made the Tanjore country flouriſh more than in Tuljagee's time. I have conſented to paying three additional battalions out of the revenues of the Tanjore country, which I was not before able to do, and the balance on their account, being two lacks ſixty odd thouſand pagodas, I agreed to pay out of the revenues of the Tanjore country only. I have paid conſiderable prize-money to the army for their trouble and fatigue, and other expences for proviſions, &c. and for the Zemindars and Collaries, who came to my aſſiſtance in great numbers. Was I to write all the expences attending theſe two expeditions, this paper would not contain them. Very large ſums have been expended in this buſineſs. It ſurpriſes and aſtoniſhes me, that the Company ſhould, *after five years*, give you this order. My ſorrow and concern on reading the Company's order are inexpreſſible; becauſe, carrying it into execution would not only be prejudicial to the honour and rights of me and my family, but alſo to the honour, juſtice, and intereſts of the Company and the Engliſh nation, and the tranquillity of the Carnatic. His Majeſty, the King of Great Britain, wrote me a letter of congratulation, in which he mentions, that my troops and the Company's have been ſucceſsful, which letter his Majeſty's plenipotentiary publicly read in my Durbar, in the preſence of all my people, and the Vaqueels of the neighbouring powers *. The king of Delhi †, and all the Hindoſtan and European powers, being convinced of my rights, ſent me letters of congratulation. Could I ſuppoſe that the Gentlemen of the Company could now diſapprove of what they had before approved of. Now, on delivering up Tanjore, what will every body ſay? Beſides, how can I provide for the payment of my creditors, who lent their money, depending upon my honour, and which I was obliged to borrow from them, to carry on the before-mentioned buſineſs? Their money depends upon me, and my dependence is on the revenues of the Tanjore country. The gentlemen of the Company have frequently written to me in favour of my creditors. You and your council are men of juſtice and wiſdom, and well acquainted with buſineſs, you yourſelves will pleaſe to judge herein. The Gentlemen of

* His Majeſty's words were, "It gave us ſatisfaction to hear, that the Governor and Council of Madras had ſent the Company's troops with yours to reduce your tributary the Raja of Tanjore to obedience; in which we hope, *by the bleſſing of God*, they will be ſucceſsful."

† Shâh Allum, the preſent Mogul emperor.

the

the Company mention in their order, that they are guarantees to the treaty of 1762, which treaty, so guaranteed, was with Pertaub Sing *only*‡. Even Pertaub Sing, by his bad conduct) as appears by a letter of his in my possession), did not merit the protection of the said guarantee. His promoting disturbances I have already mentioned to you, as also to Governor Palk, in a letter dated the 4th Junaudelowell, or 30th October 1764; Tuljagee (according to the custom of this country) is not included in the said guarantee. If you consider his disobedience and disturbances, and his selling and mortgaging some districts of his country to Europeans, who are enemies to the English interest and mine, you may judge whether the taking of Tanjore was just or not.—You may besides consider, if (supposing Tuljagee guaranteed in 1762 as well as his father) he did not lose all right to such guarantee by his conduct, because he destroyed the guarantee by drawing his sword §.

The Gentlemen of the Company, in their letter of the 17th March 1769, wrote as follows:

" It appears most unreasonable to us, that the Raja of Tanjore should " take possession of the most fruitful part of the country, which can alone " supply our armies with subsistence, and not contribute to the defence " of the Carnatic. We observe the Nabob makes very earnest repre- " sentations to you on this subject in his letter, entered in the book of " country correspondence, wherein he takes notice, that the Zemindars of " the Carnatic have been supported, and their countries preserved to them, " by the operations of our forces employed in his cause; and that nothing " was more notorious, than that three former Princes of the Carnatic had " received from the Tanjore Raja 70, 80, nay even 100 lacks of rupees at " a time; that to the preceding Nizam he had paid a contribution of 50 " lacks, and the present, if he had met with success against our army, would " not have been content with less than a crore of rupees from this Raja. " How just does it then appear, that he should be made to bear some part " of the expence of these measures, to which he owes his security and the

‡ It could not be otherwise; as the succession of his son was eventual, and depended on the favour of his feudal Lord, the Nabob of Arcot.

§ What answer can the Directors who signed the orders make to these facts?

"peace of his country? We therefore *enjoin you* to give the Nabob ſuch
"ſupport, in his pretenſions on the Raja of Tanjore, as may be effectual;
"and if the Raja *refuſes** to contribute a juſt proportion to the expence of
"the war, you are then to purſue ſuch meaſures as the Nabob may think
"conſiſtent with the juſtice and dignity of his government †."

I am a true friend to the Company, and an old friend to you alſo, and I truſt the proſperity of my affairs to you. Though it is not conſiſtent with the former promiſes of the Governor and Council that I ſhould take a Company's garriſon into Tanjore, I am willing to receive them as my beſt friends, in the ſame manner as in the fort of Trichinopoly, to pay the expence of the garriſon, and to ſhew the moſt friendly treatment to the country, and to the Company, and to increaſe the allowance of Tuljagee and his family ‡.

I have entruſted to the protection of the Company, my life, and that of my ſons, and all my family, and entirely depended on their friendſhip, and am living in their ſettlement at Madras; then how could I refuſe to give up the fort, which is compoſed only of ſtones and bricks? But what anſwer can I ſay about reſtoring to Tuljagee the fort and country of Tanjore, as it will be extremely prejudicial to my rights and honour.

I am obliged to the Gentlemen of the Company, and it is due only to their friendſhip and aſſiſtance that I have poſſeſſed my rights. I have never harboured a ſuſpicion that they would infringe my rights on *falſe* and *groundleſs reports*. I underſtand, from your Lordſhip's repreſentation, that ſhould I not comply with the Company's order, relative to Tanjore, it will be hurtful to the affairs of my government, and that the Gentlemen of the Company will be diſpleaſed with me. When by taking a garriſon of their troops into the Fort of Tanjore, I put a power in their hands, by which

* Which he did.

† Theſe Orders form a ſtriking contraſt to thoſe of the 12th of April 1775. In the latter, the Directors aſſert, with inexcuſable temerity, that the attack and capture of Tanjore was contrary to their repeated orders and inſtructions.

‡ How will Lord Pigot anſwer to this nation, for not accepting ſuch juſt, equitable, and advantageous offers? How will the *preſent* Court of Directors anſwer to the King, parliament, and people of Great Britain, for not receiving ſtill more advantageous propoſals than thoſe? *Quos deus vult perdere prius dementit.*

they

they may always act according to their pleasure, and only wish that they would, through their favour, consider my rights and do me justice; how can they be offended with me!

I have, my Lord, a long time since gained the friendship of the Company, from my father having given up his life for them; and from having been plundered of our fortune and effects acquired in a series of years; and from spending my youth with them. This friendship I regard, as the most valuable acquisition. I hope you will (through your favour) shew mercy to my old age and white hairs.

As the Gentlemen of the Company have left the management of the Tanjore business to your Lordship's wisdom, abilities, and honour, you have it in your power to represent fully to them the bad conduct and enmity of Tuljagee, my right to take the fort and country of Tanjore, my consent to receiving a Company's garrison therein, as in Trichinopoly, &c. and my desire of increasing the allowance of Tuljagee and his family.

I will give Tuljagee his liberty before I receive the garrison of my friends into the Fort of Tanjore. He shall owe that favour to me, as he is my subject. I am much in debt to my troops, and have given many orders on that country for large sums of money, which I borrowed on account of it; therefore I hope, that your Lordship will do me the favour to give orders to your officers, that they may not interfere in any respect that may disturb me in the management of the country, till a fresh order arrives from the Company. Your Lordship will much oblige me by giving these orders, and I will receive your garrison into the Fort."

The proposals offered by the Nabob, in the preceding letter are so explicit, so just and equitable, that they require no comment, and stand in need of no commendation. The conduct of lord Pigot, and the orders upon which he proceeded, are as contrary to the common prudence, as they are to true policy. A faithful ally of Great Britain, found himself obliged to displace a profligate renter of one of his provinces, because he not only refused to perform his feudal duties, but even entered into treaties with the enemies of this kingdom, as well as the Carnatic; yet the Court of Directors, under the influence of a *pretended* fit of humanity, do an act of injustice; and give back to a man, who has been uniformly the enemy of the Company, the

power

power of doing them more harm. Can any friend of Great Britain hesitate where to draw the line whom to prefer, if preference was necessary? Or where justice is only desired for whom to decide?

The Nabob still continuing ill, the following conference was held between his two sons and Lord Pigot.

Translation of a Conference between Umdaht-ul-Omrah, Ameer-ul-Omrah, and Lord Pigot, dated the second Zehige 1189 *Hegira, or 24th January* 1776.

OMDAHT-ul-Omrah and Ameer-ul-Omrah Behawders, went this morning to Lord Pigot to the Company's garden, by order of his Highness, and told him, that the Nabob was not well, and that they had left the Doctors with him; that after he had delivered the draught of his Lordship's letter to his Counsellors and Moonheer's, he had desired them to shew him a copy of his letter to the Governor and Council of the day before yesterday; and that after he had read it, he would send an answer to his Lordship to-morrow morning. His Lordship said, Why is it necessary for his Highness to peruse the copy? the letter he wrote me yesterday he should forget, as it is not a proper one for him to write*; his Highness should only write in two lines, that he will receive the Company's garrison into the fort of Tanjore, and that he will give an order to his officer commanding there to that purpose; that if his Highness would not do so, it will not be in his (his Lordship's) power to do any service to him. They replied, that the Nabob had agreed to receive the Company's garrison into the fort of Tanjore, as he had written in his letter, and what could his Lordship want more; and that his Lordship should write only two lines in answer, as his Highness had no objection to receiving the garrison. Lord Pigot replied, that the Nabob's letter was not fit to be entered in the *Company's book* †, or to be answered by him ‡. Omdaht-ul-Omrah then told him, that they would, to-morrow morning,

* It is hard, if an ally of the King of Great Britain is precluded from remonstrating against the injustice of his Majesty's own subjects.

† His Lordship appears to be in some measure sensible, that the arguments and facts contained in the letter were not much in favour of the *sovereign* authority, which *those* who *lead* the Company wish by their orders to establish in their own persons.

‡ His Lordship seems to be sensible, that the letter *could not be answered* by him.

morning, bring an anſwer from the Nabob to what his Lordſhip ſaid. Lord Pigot told him, that it gave him concern that the Nabob placed no confidence in him, and would not attend to his advice on this ſubject; and what did it ſignify their bringing the ſame anſwer to-morrow morning. That his Lordſhip had received a letter from Mr. Haſtings, congratulating him on his arrival here, and mentioning the affair of Baſalet Jung, brother to the Nizam; and that his Lordſhip having ſo much buſineſs on his hands, had not time to write an anſwer to Mr. Haſtings's letter; that he wanted to ſettle the Tanjore buſineſs, and to write the *pleaſing news* § of having done ſo to Bengal; that if he could not do ſo, he would write to Mr. Haſtings, that it gave him great concern that the Nabob would not comply with his wiſhes, by which his Highneſs's diſpleaſure appeared; that the whole country and the Company's Jaghier were in the Nabob's power; and that the ſituation of the Governor and Council here was ſuch, that they would be ſtarved if the Nabob did not furniſh them with money, as they had not got any; that in this caſe Mr. Haſtings muſt ſupply them with money from Bengal to carry on this buſineſs *. They told his Lordſhip, that they were much ſurpriſed that, conſidering the Nabob's friendſhip, he ſhould allow ſuch thoughts to enter his mind, and aſked, Who is here to fight with your Lordſhip? we only explain our ſituation to your Lordſhip, and agree to take the Company's garriſon into the fort without any objection. They then took their leave and returned to his Highneſs, and told him, that Lord Pigot wanted that his Highneſs ſhould give him leave to return his letter. His Highneſs told them, that he was very ill, that Doctor Boſwell and Doctor Storey were with him; notwithſtanding which, he would give orders to his Moonſhee to ſhew him the draught of his letter to his Lordſhip, either in the evening or at night, and that after he had read it he would ſend an anſwer to-morrow morning.

They went again the ſame morning, and told him, that the Nabob was very ill, and had taken phyſic; that Doctor Boſwell and Doctor Storey

§ This *pleaſing news* he did not chuſe to write, till a *requiſitorial letter* came from Bengal; which ſhall be printed in this collection.

* This is plainly threatening the Nabob with a war; Lord Pigot having declared, that he would ſend for money to Bengal to take Tanjore by force.

were with him; that they had explained to him his Lordſhip's meſſage; and that his Highneſs ſaid, though he was very ill, he had ordered his Moonſhee to be ready to ſhew him the draught of the letter, either in the evening or at night; and that he would ſend an anſwer to-morrow morning. His Lordſhip anſwered, that he could not have any longer patience; that he had promiſed his Council that he would ſettle this buſineſs this morning. They replied, that their father's health was ſuch, and the impatience of their uncle (meaning Lord Pigot) was ſo great, that they were in great difficulty how to act. His Lordſhip ſaid, he did not underſtand to-day or to-morrow morning; that to-morrow morning his Highneſs would not attend to his propoſal, but would ſend the ſame anſwer; that he (his Lordſhip) was going to ſend *for money to Bengal* †. They aſked him, Why are you going to ſend for money to Bengal, who is to fight with you? Your Lordſhip *may kill* any of the Nabob's family that you pleaſe, he will ſay nothing againſt it. Lord Pigot anſwered, he would not delay any longer to manage the Company's buſineſs; that the Nabob ſhould *forget* the letter he had written; that his Highneſs ſhould write, in two lines, that he would receive the Company's garriſon into Tanjore, and that he would give orders to his officers to that purpoſe, and that his Highneſs ſhould not mention any thing about the Country, &c. but that he ſhould forget the letter he had written to him, as it was a very *bad letter*; and that his Highneſs ſhould, through favour, leave this buſineſs to him; and that he (his Lordſhip) would write a *very good letter*. They replied, that they would bring his lordſhip an anſwer to-morrow morning. His Lordſhip ſaid, this delay has happened by ſaying to-day and to-morrow morning, and that it appeared they would put off the ſhip from ſailing, by to-day or to-morrow morning; that he would not allow buſineſs to be delayed in ſuch a manner; that he would immediately go to their father, and aſk him one queſtion, Whether he would do the buſineſs or not; and that he ſhould not put it off any longer. Omdaht-ul-Omrah and Ameer-ul Omrah then talked together in Perſian, obſerving that his Lordſhip talked in an extraordinary manner; for though the Nabob had written plainly, yet Lord Pigot expected a letter from him; and that his Lordſhip's real meaning ſeemed to be this, that his Highneſs ſhould not write

† To levy war on an unoffending ally of Great Britain!

any letter or desire any promise from him, before he had taken the Company's garrison into the fort; that he would do what he thought proper afterwards, but no promise now. His Lordship said, that he would come to the Nabob's house, and stay there till he finished this business. They told him that the house was *his*, but that it would be unnecessary for him to do so. His lordship said, it was very necessary for him to settle this business; that if the Nabob refused it, he would write to the Company that the Nabob was an *enemy to them*, and that he would regard him as such. They told his Lordship that the Nabob regarded the Company's friendship more than his life, and that these harsh words were an injury to his Highness. His lordship said, suppose them *harsh* or *smooth*, I must do the business; if the Nabob chooses he may write a letter as long as the room, but it will be of no advantage to this business, and I will not stir to-morrow morning till it is settled. They then took their leave, and his lordship gave them a letter from Mr. Hastings, addressed to his Highness, which they delivered to him."

On the 25th of January, the Nabob was *forced* to send the following note to Lord Pigot.

Letter from the Nabob to Lord Pigot, dated 25th January, 1776.

Chepauck, January 25th, 1776.

I Have perused the STRICT order of the Company given to my Friend, and have written a reply thereto in mine of the 22d instant, THAT AGREEABLE TO THAT I HAVE CONSENTED, AND that I have given permission for their garrison to be put in Tanjore. Fifteen days hence you may send your people, and I shall withdraw my own supernumerary people *.

His Lordship returned the following answer.

Letter from Lord Pigot to his Highness the Nabob, 25th January, 1776.

To the Nabob.

May it please your Highness,

I Am to thank your Highness for the mark you have, by your letter of this day, given of your steady friendship for my employers, the East India

* To the words in *capitals* the Nabob *did not* consent.

Company,

Company, by complying with the orders I have received from them, to put a garrison into Tanjore; and although it was impossible for me to receive that place on any conditions, yet you may be assured of every mark of my attention to your interest, so far as shall be consistent with the Company's orders.

I have the honour to be,
Your Highness's most obedient,
and most humble servant,

Fort St. George,
25th January, 1776.

PIGOT.

The following answer was returned, next day, by the Nabob.

Translation of a Letter from the Nabob to Lord Pigot, dated 4th Zebige, 1189 Hegira, or 26th January, 1776.

I Have received your Lordship's note, dated the 25th Instant.

In my answer, dated the 29th Zecaud, or 22d Instant, to your Lordship's Letter, I wrote to you in regard to Tanjore, and have great hopes of the prosperity of my affairs, from the favour and justice of the Gentlemen of the Company and you, who are my friend; and my whole dependence is on them and you.

I hope you will shew favour to my rights."

The Nabob renewed his solicitations to Lord Pigot on the 3d of February.

Translation of a Letter from his Highness the Nabob to Lord Pigot, February 3d, 1776, or 12th Zebige 1189 Hegira.

I Understand, from your intimation, the desire of the Gentlemen of the Company to have a garrison in the Fort of Tanjore. As I have been from the beginning their true friend, and invariable well-wisher, and as they are bound to protect my honour, and to secure my country and my rights, and are assistants to me in all my affairs; as they, my best friends, have had all my strong forts put under their care by me, and I have, through friendship, considered our interests as the same; therefore, except to explain my situation

tion and my rights, I have *not opposed* their intention in any respect; but have, with great integrity of heart and great friendship, wrote in my letter to you, dated the 29th Zecaud 1189 Hegira, or 22d of January 1776, that the Fort of Tanjore might be kept in the care of my friends; and therefore send the inclosed order to Mahommed Nagif Cawn, Bahauder, to deliver up the Fort to the care of my friends, whereby I have given to the whole world a proof of the sentiments of my heart, which is filled with friendship for the Company and the English nation. I am entirely convinced, that you will represent to the Gentlemen of the Company, my friendship and regard to them, in the same colours as you have seen them with your own eyes. And I have strong hopes, that you will (through your favour) give orders to the officer whom you appoint to the command of the Fort of Tanjore, to preserve the honour of my representatives and servants, and act jointly with them, and not to obstruct the business of the country, but to give his assistance in it."

Lord Pigot, eager to accomplish his views, paid no attention to the supplications of the Nabob. The following laconic note was received, by that prince, on the day it was written.

Translation of a Note from Lord Pigot to the Nabob, dated 3d Mohurrum 1190 Hegira, or 23d February 1776.

I Want to know how many orders are given for the payment of the money on the Tanjore country, and what person the Nabob thinks proper to be deputed *from me* to settle the business of Tanjore.'

Lord Pigot, on the same day, sent a copy of the following paper to the Nabob.

What the President, Lord Pigot, wanted the Nabob to agree to.

THE President acquaints the Board, that the Nabob has delivered to him a paper, containing the amount of the orders he has given upon the Tanjore country. That the Nabob has likewise given him an order, directed to all his Hamildars, &c. commanding them to account with such persons as he, *the President, may name*, for all the sums collected in the Tanjore country *since the 9th instant* *; and directing the said Hamildars, &c. to relinquish all manner of authority, should they be required by him so to do.

The President thinks, therefore, the Company's orders may *now* be carried into effect †; and that the Raja should be placed in the full possession and management of the country, by a public order to all the Hamildars, &c.

The safety of Tanjore, and the security of the Raja and his family, appearing to make it necessary, that an English garrison should not only be in the Fort, but the country also be protected by the Company's troops, the President recommends, that the Raja be requested to permit the same; and to allot for this purpose a sum not exceeding the amount of what he formerly paid to his own troops.

The safety of the Carnatic depends upon a well-disciplined force, regularly paid, being kept up. The particular safety and quiet of every individual seems to require, that no other force should be permitted to be kept up; and these considerations induce the Board to wish that the Raja would join them in their endeavours to place the country in this situation.

In order to induce the Nabob to assent hereto, the Raja may be *desired* to allow the amount of the several orders the Nabob has given upon the Tanjore country to be discharged out of the Revenues thereof.

The provision thus made towards the support of the army by the Raja of Tanjore, will render it unnecessary for the Nabob, in time of peace, to be at a greater expence than the sum the Company now charge him with, and such of his regiments of horse as have been long in his service, and he is desirous of having continued in pay, may be kept up without putting him to that expence.

* Why his Lordship should fix on the 9th of February as the day of commencing *his* receipt of the revenue of Tanjore merits *explanation.* He had arrived in the first week of December. He had in his pocket *positive Orders* for giving back Tanjore to the Raja. Why has he delayed their execution so long? Had he negociations at Madras which took up all his time? It is believed he had. But men *unacquainted* with his Lordship will say: "Either the orders were *just* "or *unjust*. If they were *just*, how could you, my Lord, defer so long their execution? if they "were *unjust*, why did you execute them at all? You had a fair opening for putting off "the business, till a further explanation should arrive from Europe?" These questions are not easily answered; and therefore an answer is not expected.

† Why might they not have been carried into effect before? Lord Pigot's Dubasch could, if he pleased, answer this question.

The Prefident adds, that having explained this to the Nabob, his Highnefs, in teftimony of his fincere friendfhip to the Company, readily *affents thereto* ‡."

The following affecting Paper was fent by the Nabob, in confequence of the preceding Paper and Note.

Tranflation of a Paper from his Highnefs to Lord Pigot, dated 6th Moburrum 1190 *Hegira, or* 26*th February* 1776.

BEFORE the reduction of Tanjore, I was not much loaded with debt, but there remained a little due to my old creditors, as I was obliged to pay ten lack of Pagodas, on account of Myfore.

On the firft expedition againft Tanjore, my eldeft fon fettled matters there, and took agreement for the payment of the money, which I affigned to my creditors; but Tuljagee was totally deficient in the payment, whereby they fuffered delay. For this reafon, and the other bad conduct of Tuljagee, which I have mentioned in my former letters, we were induced to fend the Company's troops and mine to take Tanjore. From Arcot, Nellore, Trichinopoly, Trinevelly, and from all my other countries, fighting people are affembled and provifions, bullocks, fheep, &c. in great quantities for the ufe of the army, were provided for this expedition.

In carrying on this bufinefs I contracted heavy debts, by raifing troops for the defence of the forts and countries which were weakened by the old troops being drawn from them to go againft Tanjore, by paying Batta to the army; and to thofe who brought affiftance, by paying prize-money to the army on both expeditions, and other expences; and by paying money to the Dutch to releafe the diftricts poffeffed by them: as all the countries belong to me, I gave orders on fuch places as I thought proper, for the payment of the faid debts, and the pay of the troops, &c. Now, your Lordfhip requires a particular account of the orders I gave on Tanjore. If I give you only an account of the orders on that country, all the debts that lie upon me and my country for the two expeditions againft Tanjore,

‡ His Highnefs had the fpirit not to *affent*. He refolved to fubmit to force, and even to indignity; but he ftood firm to his rights.

and

and the money paid to the Dutch, will be loſt.—In this caſe, how am I to write you only an account of the orders given on the Tanjore country? Should any hindrance happen in the affairs of that country, the clamours of my creditors and my troops will be very loud; conſidering which, I beg of your Lordſhip to excuſe me on this ſubject (as I deſired in my letter of the 29th of Zecaud, or 22d of January laſt), till you receive a further order from the Company. I now again beg the ſame favour.—I have cheerfully received the garriſon of my friends in the Fort of Tanjore, and am ready (till the further order arrives) to increaſe Tuljagee's allowance, and to pay the expence of the garriſon in any manner you think proper, and may write me.

If Tuljagee had not obliged me to undertake thoſe two expeditions againſt Tanjore, I ſhould by this time have been maſter of much treaſure.—I took Tanjore thinking that my honour, the honour of the King of Great Britain, the Company, and the Engliſh nation, and of the Governor and Council, were concerned, and that it was my right to take it. Had I foreſeen the difficulties that attend this buſineſs before we took Tanjore, though the tranquillity of the Carnatic was much diſturbed, and our intereſts ſuffered by it, we would not have had any thing to do with it. I am therefore under great ſorrow and uneaſineſs, and put myſelf under your protection. It is worthy of your long friendſhip, that you ſhould take by the hand your *old friend*, who is *ſinking in the whirlpool*, and give him protection *."

The Nabob ſent alſo the following anſwer to Lord Pigot's note and paper of February the 23d.

Tranſlation of a Letter from his Highneſs the Nabob to Lord Pigot, dated 7th Mohurrum 1190 *Hegira, or 27th February* 1776.

IN anſwer to your Lordſhip's requeſt of the 23d of February 1776, or 3d Mohurrum 1100 Hegira, to be informed, what order I had given on the Tanjore country, and what perſon I wiſhed to be ſent on a deputation thither;

* Application to the *weaker* paſſions have little effect, when the *ſtrong* prevail. His Lordſhip only can determine which of his paſſions is the *ſtrongeſt*, at *his* age. One would have thought, that the ſtate is too feeble to *defend* its allies, when ſuch an humiliating application is made in vain to the repreſentative of a company of Traders.

thither; I ſent you by my two ſons a paper, containing my opinion on the 26th February. Upon this, your Lordſhip ſent me, by Mr. Chambers, a paper written in *your own hand* for my peruſal. The contents of that paper ſurpriſed me much; from the time in which a garriſon of my friends has been put in Tanjore, I have repeatedly explained to your Lordſhip, as in my letter of the 22d January, my ſentiments relative to my rights, and the difficulties that would ariſe from interfering with the buſineſs of the country. I now write your Lordſhip, that I *did not* explain to you my ſentiments in the manner you have been pleaſed to write in the paper, ſent by Mr. Chambers. I beg your Lordſhip may write me what you propoſe to ſay on this ſubject. I will in return, write your Lordſhip my ſentiments plainly. I always regard my good friends, the Company, as the protectors of my honour, my reputation, and my family."

Lord Pigot endeavoured to *obtain* the following paper from the Nabob. But the Nabob *never conſented*, either to the paper or the propoſals it contains.

A Paper ſent by Lord Pigot to his Highneſs the Nabob 26th February 1776, *or 6th Mohurrum* 1190 *Hegira.*

THE Preſident acquaints the Board, that the Nabob has delivered to him a paper, containing the amount of the orders he has given upon the Tanjore country. That the Nabob has likewiſe given him an order, directed to all his Amildars, &c. commanding them to account with ſuch perſons as he, the Preſident, may name, for all ſums collected in the Tanjore country, ſince the 9th inſtant; and directing the ſaid Amildars, &c. to relinquiſh all manner of authority, ſhould they be required by him ſo to do *.

The Preſident thinks, therefore, the Company's orders may *now* be carried into effect †; and that the Raja ſhould be placed in the full poſſeſſion and management of the country, by a public order to all the Amildars, &c.

* No ſuch order was ever given.

† Why were they not carried into effect before? Were the *preparations* neceſſary for the *reſtoration* at Tanjore ſo important, that, on their account, the *poſitive orders* of the Company muſt be ſuſpended?

The

The ſafety of Tanjore, and the *ſecurity of the Raja and his family* ‡, appearing to make it neceſſary, that an Engliſh garriſon ſhould not only be in the Fort, but the country alſo be protected by the Company's troops, the Preſident recommends, that the Raja *be requeſted* § to permit the ſame, and to allot for this purpoſe a ſum not exceeding the amount of what he formerly paid to his own troops.

The ſafety of the Carnatic depends upon a well-diſciplined force regularly paid being kept up: the particular ſafety and quiet of every individual ſeems to require, that no other ſhould be permitted to be kept up; and theſe conſiderations induce the Board to wiſh, that the Raja would join them in their endeavours to place the country in this ſituation.

In order to induce the Nabob to aſſent hereto, the Raja may be deſired to allow the amount of the ſeveral orders the Nabob has given upon the Tanjore country, to be diſcharged out of the revenues thereof *.

The proviſion thus made towards the ſupport of the army by the Raja of Tanjore, will render it unneceſſary for the Nabob, in time of peace, to be at a greater expence, than the ſum the Company now charge him with; and ſuch of his regiments of horſe as have been long in his ſervice, and he is deſirous of having continued in pay, may be kept up, without putting him to that expence.

The Preſident adds, that having explained this to the Nabob, his Highneſs, in teſtimony of his ſincere friendſhip to the Company, readily aſſents thereto †.

Received 6th Mohurrum 1190 Hegira,
or 26th February 1776."

The Nabob complains, in the following letter, of Lord Pigot's unfairneſs, in the preceding paper.

‡ This inſinuates a ſuſpicion of the Nabob, which has been already diſproved by facts.

§ Pretty language to a *man of ſtraw*, from the repreſentative of a body of men who diſpoſe of kingdoms with the daſh of a pen!

* Lord Pigot afterwards changed his mind; but he was out-voted by his Council, who diſapproved of *all* his proceedings at Tanjore.

† His Highneſs never gave his aſſent.

Tranſlation

Translation of a Letter from his Highness the Nabob to Lord Pigot, dated 7th Mohurrum 1190 *Hegira, or 27th February* 1776.

IN anſwer to your Lordſhip's requeſt of the 23d February 1776, or 3d Mohurrum 1190 Hegira, to be informed what orders I had given on the Tanjore country, and what perſon I wiſhed to be ſent on a deputation thither: I ſent you by my two ſons, a paper containing my opinion on the 26th February: upon this, your Lordſhip ſent me, by Mr. Chambers, a paper written in your own hand for my peruſal. The contents of that paper ſurpriſed me much.—From the time in which a garriſon of my friends had been put in Tanjore, I have repeatedly explained to your Lordſhip, as in my letter of the 22d January, my ſentiments relative to my rights, and the difficulties that would ariſe from interfering with the buſineſs of the country. I now write your Lordſhip, that I did *not* explain to you my ſentiments in the manner you have been pleaſed to write in the paper ſent by Mr. Chambers.—I beg your Lordſhip may write me what *you* propoſe to ſay on this ſubject. I will, in return, write your Lordſhip my ſentiments plainly. I always regard my good friends the Company, as the protectors of my honour, my reputation, and my family.

The following is Lord Pigot's anſwer to the Nabob's letter of the 26th February.

Copy of a Letter from Lord Pigot, to his Highneſs the Nabob, dated the 6th March 1776.

I Have received your Highneſs's Letter of the 26th February, in which you repreſent to me the very great diſtreſs of your finances, by the expences you have incurred on account of the Tanjore expeditions. Turn your own thoughts towards a remedy, and I can aſſure you, that no aſſiſtance, which is conſiſtent with the orders of my maſters, ſhall be omitted, on my part, to relieve you from every diſtreſs.

The orders I have received from the Company, are to reſtore the country of Tanjore to the Raja; but ſuch has been my ſolicitude to do every thing in concert with your Highneſs, that this is *yet* unexecuted, notwithſtanding that an Engliſh garriſon has been almoſt a month in Tanjore *.

* This is but a lame excuſe for his Lordſhip's delay.

Humanity to the wretched inhabitants, diſtreſſed beyond meaſure, by the miſerable ſtate in which the country now remains, without any eſtabliſhed government, either of your Highneſs † or the Raja; juſtice to the Raja, who is ſcarcely better than a priſoner ſtill ‡, and attention to the public honour, make it abſolutely neceſſary to carry into immediate effect the orders of the Company.

I muſt therefore beg leave to repeat my requeſt, that you will give an order, directed to all your Hamildars, &c. in the Tanjore country, to relinquiſh all manner of authority when called upon by me ſo to do, and to account with ſuch perſons as *I may name*, for all ſums collected in the Tanjore country, from the day I had the honour to deliver the Company's letter to your Highneſs.

I beg alſo that you will be pleaſed to give me the amount of the orders, you have given on the Tanjore country.

I have the honour to be
Your Highneſs's
moſt obedient humble ſervant,

Fort St. George,
6th March 1776.

(Signed) PIGOT.

Lord Pigot writes a paper to *himſelf*, and deſires the Nabob to father it. Upon this the following conference was held.

Tranſlation of a Conference between the Nabob and Lord Pigot, March 18th, 1776.

LORD Pigot came to his Highneſs about ten o'clock this morning, and explained to him, by Mr. Chambers, a paper which he deſired that his Highneſs ſhould write to him. His Highneſs told his Lordſhip, that he would write him to-morrow what he wiſhed to ſay to him.

† He himſelf had deſtroyed the Nabob's government; and here he complains of his own act.

‡ It is remarkable, that the Company's commanding officer at Tanjore conſidered the Raja as a priſoner, after the Nabob had delivered up the Fort. The Nabob offered to ſet the Raja at large, *before* he admitted a garriſon into Tanjore; yet Lord Pigot rejected that propoſal; and notwithſtanding the *ſtrict orders of his Maſters*, (to uſe his own words) kept him ſtill a priſoner. Here ſomething " more was meant than meets the ear." Had Tuljagee been ſet at liberty before his Lordſhip's arrival at Tanjore, he might *forget* the favour.

Translation of a Paper which Lord Pigot desires that his Highness the Nabob should write to him, received the 28th Mokurrum 1190 Hegira, or 19th March 1776.

IN answer to your Lordship's Letter in regard to the country of Tanjore, I inform you, that I did not take that country from the Raja until his disobedience was so evident to the Company, the whole world, and to me, that we were convinced he deserved chastisement. Therefore I cannot return that country to him; but it is not my desire that even my enemy should despond of receiving the favour that the Company wish to shew him; for I am well convinced that in shewing him that favour, my friends will attend to preserving my honour and the interests of the Carnatic; wherefore I will cheerfully deliver the country of Tanjore into the hands of the Company, provided my sovereignty therein may be assured to me. For these purposes I have sent the necessary orders. *The Raja will be always disobedient* *; *his nature leads him to this:* I should therefore have a strong agreement from him not to entertain troops in future, for I should otherwise be obliged to punish him again. It is also my wish that such a part of the revenues of the Tanjore country should be set aside for the Company as may be sufficient for the payment of the troops which they may appoint there for its security, and for the defence of the Carnatic. I consent to all this, from my intention that the Company may have the most evident proof of my firm friendship to them, and to convince them that I consider their advantage as my own. This is the strongest test of my friendship. I therefore trust that my friends will not leave on me the present burden of my debts. The pressing distresses of my finances are too clear to require my enumerating them to your Lordship. I only mention this, that their rise have been principally due to the desire of me and my family to assist my friends. However, the business has succeeded well, and I am happy in the remembrance of it. My sons will follow my example. God has pleased to give me many sons, and he has, through his divine favour, given them another father (which is the Company), and I commit them to their protection.

* This is a strange character given of the Raja, by the very man who restores him! If he is a dangerous and profligate man, how can Lord Pigot, how can those who gave the orders, answer for having placed the power of doing harm, in his hands?

Contrary to Lord Pigot's wiſhes, the Nabob adheres with ſpirit to his undoubted rights. But, at the ſame time that he is determined to ſupport his own rights, he makes offers and conceſſions to the Company, which the world will not juſtify his Lordſhip in rejecting. The whole conduct of Lord Pigot ſeems more calculated to mortify and oppreſs the Nabob, than to ſerve his Maſters. It is ſaid he has *effectually* ſerved *himſelf*. There is not a ſingle fact advanced in the following letter, that cannot be proved from the Records of the Company. Their conduct, therefore, to their old friend and benefactor, is replete with ingratitude as well as injuſtice.

Tranſlation of a Letter from his Highneſs the Nabob to Lord Pigot, dated 19*th March* 1776, *or* 28*th Mohurrum* 1190 *Hegira.*

I Have received your Lordſhip's letter of the 6th inſtant, in which you are pleaſed to ſay, in anſwer to my repreſentation of the great diſtreſs of my finances, from the two expeditions againſt Tanjore, that I ſhould turn my thoughts towards a remedy, and that no aſſiſtance, which is conſiſtent with the orders of your Maſters, ſhall be omitted on your part to relieve me from every diſtreſs; for which I am obliged to you.

If your Lordſhip is reſolved, notwithſtanding my repreſentations and requeſts, both to you and the Company, about the country of Tanjore, to give it to Tuljagee, to what remedy ſhall I turn my thoughts?

I have not contracted my debts by *ſpending money in oſtentation* and *uſeleſs purſuits*; but I have contracted them in the national war againſt Madras, in the reduction of Pondicherry, and the expedition againſt Madura †; in the diſturbances made by the Nizam, when the Company took poſſeſſion of the Circars, and afterwards by their taking the Dewanſhip of Myſore, and making an expedition againſt that country, which occaſioned Hyder Aly to enter the Carnatic, and plunder it as he thought proper, which put me to great expence, as well for the ſupport of the Company's army as my own.

† Lord Pigot is no ſtranger to the particulars of that expedition; it is alſo ſaid, that his Lordſhip was in correſpondence with Iſouf Cawn; but this was *before* that partiſan rebelled; Colonel Monſon, now a member of the Supreme Council at Bengal, can, when he pleaſes, refreſh his Lordſhip's memory on this ſubject.

All

All these things have *not* been brought on by me ‡, as I have already mentioned in my letter dated the 2d Showall 1183 Hegira, to the Governor and Council. My debts have been also increased by my paying ten lacks of Pagodas, on account of the Mysore expedition, which I had no right to pay. All these expences have been incurred by me for the assistance of my friends, and I am happy in the remembrance of it. I have paid off great part, and very little now remains. If the before-mentioned affairs had not happened, I should not owe any thing; the money which I was obliged to borrow for the reduction of Tanjore was with a view to preserve the tranquillity of the Carnatic, and to assure the general peace and safety. If I had not done so, what disturbances would not have happened in this country from the bad conduct of Tuljagee, his application to the Marattas for assistance, and to the Dutch and other powers, as I have set forth in my letters to your Lordship of the 22d January and 26th February last * ? I can clearly explain

‡ No. The servants of the Company *brought on* the wars, and the Nabob bore the expences.

* Though the Court of Directors have shewn so much favour to Tuljagee, the following facts are incontrovertible. In compliance with his solicitations, twenty thousand Marratto horse appeared on the frontiers of the Carnatic under the command of Trimbuckrow, in the year 1772, and threatened the whole country with fire and sword. To gratify these marauders, the Nabob was obliged to pay down a considerable sum of money, besides presents of jewels, fire-arms, and elephants. The intercepted letters of Tuljagee to Poonah prove, that this invasion was undertaken by his advice, and at his instigation.

Though the Marattos retreated, contrary to the expectations of the Raja of Tanjore, he continued his intrigues at Poonah. In the beginning of the year 1773, he sent a person to that capital, to entertain a body of horse, and to solicit the alliance of the State for a war against the Carnatic. Mr. Mostyn, the English Resident at the Court of Poonah, was no stranger to this negociation. He advised the Governor and Council of Fort St. George, that the Carnatic was to be invaded by the combined forces of the Marattos and the Raja. The Nabob, as well as the Company's servants, being averse to a fresh war, perhaps delayed too long the only effectual means to deprive Tuljagee of the power of injury.

It is evident, from the whole tenor of Tuljagee's conduct, from the day the first siege of Tanjore was raised, that he meditated another war. He only waited for a fit opportunity of carrying fire and sword through the dominions of the Nabob, his lawful and acknowledged superior. Happily for the prosperity of the Carnatic, fortunately for the English, the abilities of the Raja were not equal to his perfidy. His intrigues, however, were not confined to Asiatic powers. Though he had sent several embassies to Hyder Ali, he turned chiefly his views to quarters still more alarming to the Nabob and the Company. He entered into the strictest connections with the French, the Dutch, and the Danes, as appeared from the original Sunnuds, delivered up to plain to your Lordſhip the nature of my debts on account of the Tanjore country, provided you do not obſtruct my management of the revenues.

Your Lordſhip has written to me, that the Company's orders to you are, to put the Tanjore country into the hands of Tuljagee, but that it is your wiſh to tranſact every buſineſs in concurrence with me; and though the Engliſh Company's garriſon has been one month in the fort of Tanjore, you have not yet complied with the orders of your Maſters. I conſider the Gentlemen of the Company as my friends, and it is by their favour and aſſiſtance that I have got poſſeſſion of my right. I am always thankful to them, and I readily received their garriſon into the fort of Tanjore, as into my other forts, to take care of it, in order that the Company might have the ſtrongeſt proof of my friendſhip towards them; yet if any one imagines that the *putting the fort into their hands, agreeing to give a ſuitable Jaghire to Tuljagee, paying the expence of the garriſon, and performing the ſame as the Company expect from Tuljagee (as I have propoſed in my letter of the 22d January), is not complying with their ſentiments, it is my misfortune* *! It is my misfortune that the Gentlemen

to the Nabob after the capture of Tanjore by the reſpective governors of thoſe three nations. He had actually concluded a treaty with the French. Large ſums of money, an excluſive privilege of trade, and valuable territories, were to have been exchanged for a body of Europeans and a train of artillery. To the Dutch he ſold ſome diſtricts, mortgaged others; and ſet aſide the Suba of Manugoody, for the expreſs purpoſe of paying a body of troops, with which they were to ſupply him in his meditated war againſt the Nabob. He mortgaged ſome other diſtricts to the Danes; and raiſed money by theſe means from their ſettlement at Tanquebar. The Dutch actually began to aſſemble troops at Nigapatnam; and their alliance with the Raja of Tanjore was openly avowed by the Governor of Batavia, in a letter to the Nabob. All the facts ſtated in this note are *proved* incontrovertibly, by original letters and papers annexed to the *State of Facts relative to Tanjore* lately publiſhed.

* I ſhould be glad to know what will the Directors, who oppoſed the ſigning of the orders for reſtoring Tanjore, ſay to Lord Pigot's rejecting theſe propoſals. How will thoſe who *ſigned them*, anſwer to their conſtituents, their Sovereign, the Parliament, and the Nation, for their conduct in this unhappy affair? What will the leaders in the India-Houſe ſay, when called upon to give an account of orders, which ſtript a faithful friend of his dominions, and gave them to an avowed enemy? Did not ten Directors vote againſt thoſe orders; and one of them enter a ſtrong proteſt againſt them? Did not the orders lie two weeks on the table before a ſufficient number of ſignatures could be obtained? Did not ſeveral of thoſe Directors, who ſigned the orders, *declare*, that they could only be induced to ſign them, by the conſideration that there was other important and

Gentlemen of the Company have not been acquainted with the free and full ſtate of affairs, even ſo much ſo, that they are aſſured that Tuljagee is at Trichinopoly. When his Majeſty, the Parliament, and the Company fully underſtand the true ſtate of affairs, they will approve of the conduct of their ally and friend here, in not conſenting to his own diſgrace, and the ruin of the future intereſt of the Company and the Engliſh nation, by eſtabliſhing his ſubjects in the Carnatic, which would be the foundation of many troubles and diſorders. I have ſet forth, in my writing to my friends the Company, all my ſituation and rights, and reminded them of their former orders in regard to Tanjore; and I do not expect from them (who are men of juſtice) that I ſhould loſe my rights. Your Lordſhip will not interfere (as I have deſired in my letter of the 22d January laſt) in my management of the country of Tanjore which belongs to me, till we hear further from the Company. Why ſhould not I lay before you the prejudice that will ariſe to my affairs, ſhould I comply with your deſire? for it would not only be attended with the loſs of the Tanjore country, but with the total confuſion of my government. Therefore I again intreat your Lordſhip, *in the name of* the *King of Great Britain*, the *Parliament*, and *the Company*, that till you receive a freſh order from the Company, you will not interfere in the management of the Tanjore country, and do me the favour to ſpare the honour of the *oldeſt* and *trueſt friend* the Engliſh ever found in India. By ſhewing me this favour, and giving me leave to explain how much it is for the good of the Company, that thoſe rights ſhould be ſupported, your Lordſhip will not only do me juſtice, but gain the higheſt approbation of your King and Nation. I am, by the bleſſing of God, the firſt Prince in Hindoſtan, for the ſupport of whoſe right the King and Nation of Great Britain have pledged the honour of their protection and guarantee.

Your Lordſhip writes, that humanity to the wretched inhabitants, diſtreſſed beyond meaſure by the miſerable ſtate in which the country now remains, without any eſtabliſhed government either of me or the Raja; juſtice to the Raja, who is ſcarcely better than a priſoner; and attention to the public honour, make it abſolutely neceſſary to carry into immediate effect the orders of the Company.

and neceſſary buſineſs contained in the public letter? As to the *pretended approval*, SURREPTITIOUSLY OBTAINED, the Reader will find that matter explained, in a manner not much to the *credit* of ſome Perſons, in the OBSERVATIONS annexed to theſe Papers.

 The

The miſerable ſituation, my Lord, of the Tanjore inhabitants, and their deſerting the country, proceeded from the *oppreſſions of Tuljagee* *, before it came into my hands. No one oppreſſed the inhabitants more than he did, and he poſſeſſed himſelf of the fortune and cattle of many of thoſe who quitted his country, and pulled down their houſes in hopes of finding money buried under them. He did not, for ſeveral years, repair the water-houſes, mounds, and tanks. After the taking of Tanjore, by ſending my ſecond ſon Ameer-ul-Omrah Behauder, by advancing money to the inhabitants for bullocks for the cultivation of the ground, promiſing to give them their ſhare of the produce, repairing the mound, water-courſes, &c. I gave ſuch encouragement to the inhabitants, that they returned from Trivancore, Myſore, &c. The Cavery river, at the ſame time, ſwelled more than it had done for ninety years before, and overflowed the country to ſuch an extreme, as to deſtroy all the Paddy fields, and to break away the mounds and water-courſes. Ameer-ul-Omrah Behauder himſelf went there, and at the expence of many lacks and great pains, compleatly repaired them, and twice made advance to the inhabitants of ready-money and Paddy for ſeed, which prevented their ruin, and ſet them again to cultivation; which they performed in ſuch a manner as had never been done in Tuljagee's time, as is well known to the whole world, now the crop is ripe, and ready for reaping, and the time for the advantage of the inhabitants is arrived, and for their giving my ſhare and taking theirs; but they have abandoned the country, by which it appears, that from the former oppreſſions of Tuljagee, they renewed their apprehenſions.

Whilſt Tuljagee was in the cuſtody of my ſervants, he paſſed his time *more happily than during his own government*, and I will not omit increaſing his allowances according to your opinion. He has been in cuſtody of the Company's people ſince their garriſon went into Tanjore. You wrote me

* Nothing could equal the diſtreſs of the province of Tanjore during Tuljagee's government. He extorted money by unheard-of tortures from the farmers. If he heard of a woman of beauty in any part of the country, ſhe was forced from her huſband, her father, or her friends, and ſubmitted to his own luſts or thoſe of the companions of his infamous pleaſures. The people fled from his oppreſſions to the neighbouring provinces, towns and villages were depopulated, and deſolation and poverty covered the whole face of the country. When the Nabob got poſſeſſion, the confidence of the people in his juſtice and humanity induced them to return. The towns and villages began to be rebuilt; cultivation was revived; but the confuſions of which Lord Pigot complains, began afreſh, when it was known that Tuljagee was to be reſtored.

that

that you repeat your requeſt, that I ſhould give an order directed to all my Hamildars, &c. in the Tanjore country, to relinquiſh all manner of authority when called upon by you ſo to do, and to account with ſuch perſons as you may name, for all ſums collected in the Tanjore country, from the day your Lordſhip delivered me the Company's order. From your firſt queſtion on this ſubject, I have been uniform in my explanation of my ſentiments in regard to the country of Tanjore which is my right, and part of the Carnatic, and I now make my requeſt to your Lordſhip as before, on this ſubject.

The Nabob having ſtrenuouſly adhered to his rights, Lord Pigot came to confer with him the day after the preceding letter was written. The conference needs no comment. The moſt remarkable paſſages are printed in *Italics*, to call the attention of the reader. Among other matters of information his Lordſhip (perhaps through inadvertence) makes the Nabob acquainted with the *true motives* of his voyage to India.

Conference between his Highneſs the Nabob and Lord Pigot, dated 20th March 1776, or 29th Mohurrum 1190 Hegira.

HIS Lordſhip came to his Highneſs about ten o'clock this morning. Nabob Shaw Hammud Jung, Omdaht-ul-Omrah, Ameer-ul-Omrah, and Syfel Mulk were preſent. His Lordſhip told his Highneſs, that his Highneſs promiſed him, on his going to England, that he would not ſhew favour to any other perſon or attend to any advice but his; that he would not ſhew favour to the Governor and Council for the time *then to come* †, as he had ſhewn to him: That his Highneſs had not obſerved this, and that he (his Lordſhip) had heard that he had ſhewn *favour* to the *governors* and *council*, and attended to the advice of *bad people*: That therefore his Highneſs's buſineſs was in confuſion: That his Lordſhip had formerly left his Highneſs in tranquillity and honour, but that he was not ſo now: That the *raſcals* who had adviſed his Highneſs to take Tanjore, now gave his Highneſs hopes of keeping it, and bad advice alſo. What good conſequence did his Highneſs find from their advice in taking Tanjore, that he ſhould expect any from their advice now to keep it? That he ſhould not

† The Governor meant was Mr. Palk.

G hope

hope that country should again be in his hands from the assistance of the people of England. That when his Lordship formerly engaged in the affairs of Tanjore, the faith of the whole nation was concerned therein *: That when he formerly left this country, *the kingdom of England was in a good situation: That after the late king died, his present majesty managed the business of his kingdom very well, lived in pleasure, and gained victories: That* ONE BAD MAN *came, and gave his advice, therefore that the business of the kingdom was ruined* ‡, *and the people of America were fallen into rebellion: That the city had given a petition to his majesty; and in the same manner his Highness's business was spoiled by the advice of bad people: That if his Highness did not do the Tanjore business, the company would think him their enemy, and that he acted in opposition to them, and had connection with the king's people* §: That he did not say, that his Highness should not express his rights, that he might strongly explain them: That his Highness might say, that the Tanjore business had been done by the approbation of the governor and council, and the king's two ministers, and that, notwithstanding, his Highness had given up the country at the desire of the Company, which would increase their friendship to him.

Ameer-ul-Omrah told his Lordship, that the Company might form suspicions against the Nabob, had he not put the Fort of Tanjore into the care of the Company, but that now he had done so, they could have none. That the country was open, and that his Lordship might do what he wanted, by *force* and *oppression*; but that the Nabob could not give his consent to destroying his own rights. His Lordship proposed the business of taking Tanjore. His Highness answered, I did; and the Company assisted me.— His Lordship said, it was his opinion, that his Highness had desired it, and that the Company had done it. He further said, that he had in England, began the business of restoring to the Raja his country, as his honour was concerned therein; that he was the beginner of this business ‖, and would go to

* That is in his treaty with *Pertaub Sing* in 1762. The *nation* knew nothing of the matter, and the *Sovereign* contradicted it in the *guarantee* of 1763.

‡ The kingdom is much obliged to his Lordship.

§ A mighty crime truly for an ally of Great Britain to have connection with the servants of the king of Great Britain.

‖ We know his Lordship was the first mover in this business. We are no strangers to his visits to the India House, and his *proper applications* to the *Leaders* of the *then* Court of Directors. Time has unveiled the intrigues and influence used upon the occasion.

England

England after he had finished it †. That the business of this place was so far confused, that it could not be settled by his hands; and that, no doubt, it was of great prejudice to him. *That the King and Parliament would do him great injury on account of this business, and would take his estate from him.* His Lordship said, my situation is as when the General of an army picks out some men and sends them to storm a place; though they are killed, it is for the general advantage.—So I am going to Tanjore, and by *ruining myself* ‡, I shall establish friendship between your Highness and the Company. His Lordship further said to his Highness, For God's sake settle my business, and give an order under your hand to the Hamildars of Tanjore. His Lordship then stood up, and reached a gum bottle, thinking there was ink in it, and took a pen out of his pocket, and laid his hands on his Highness's feet, and his Highness laid his hands on his Lordship's feet. The young Nabobs told his Lordship, that he was as a father to them, and begged that he would spare them in this business: that he had power and might do what he pleased. His Lordship perceiving that what he had said had not effect, sat down again, and told his Highness that he might be assured, that the friendship between him and the Company would be lessened, and that he (his Lordship) wished to increase it; and that the report which had prevailed of his Highness's withdrawing his confidence from the Company, and placing it in the *Minister's and King's people* might be removed; and that his Highness's goodness and reputation might be talked of. That when his Lordship had formerly departed for England, his Highness was a great Prince; and that when his Highness used to go to Tanjore, the Raja sent his sons and other ambassadors to him with presents; and that when his Highness went farther, the Rajas of Nallacoty, Tondyman, and other Polygars, used to do the same; but that if he was to go there now, it would be some Conocoplys * bringing plantains that would come. That his Highness said, that he would lose his honour, but that he (his Lordship) said it would be increased. His Highness got up in great concern, and went into another room. His Lordship said, that as some people were blown up by the springing of a mine, so should he, for that the King and the Parliament would *cut off his head*; and that his house would be destroyed. Nevertheless, he would go and settle the Tanjore business, as he had un-

† Here his Lordship avows, that it was only to restore Tanjore he went to India.

‡ Credat Judæus.

* Inferiour Servants.

dertaken

dertaken it, let what would happen afterwards: that his Highneſs might remember this. Ameer-ul-Omrah told his Lordſhip, that if a man had committed a fault, and was to have his *head cut off*; if he aſked a little time, it would be given to him. That the Nabob was a true friend to the Company and the Engliſh nation, and had done the Tanjore buſineſs by the approbation of the Company, the Governor and Council, and now waited for an anſwer from the ſame Company; and now requeſted, that his Lordſhip would ſtay till it arrived: that it was ſurpriſing that his Lordſhip would not agree to it. His Lordſhip ſaid, that if any delay happened in this buſineſs, the people of England would think that he could not do it, and would ſend Mr. *Rumbold* here.—His Highneſs then returned from the room, and his Lordſhip took a paper out of his pocket and ſhewed it to him. It mentioned, that the Nabob would not agree to the order about Tanjore; therefore that his Lordſhip was going there, and intended to ſend Sepoys there. His Highneſs ſaid, why will your Lordſhip ſend Sepoys there? that country belongs to your *friend* not to your *enemy!*

The following is Lord Pigot's anſwer to the Nabob's letter of the 19th March. His Lordſhip deſerts the argument, and has recourſe to the poſitive orders of his *Maſters.*

Copy of a Letter from Lord Pigot to the Nabob, dated 22d March 1776.

To the Nabob.

I Have had the honour to receive your Highneſs's letter, dated the 19th inſtant, and after having paid the moſt reſpectful attention to every argument you have been pleaſed to enforce, I find myſelf obliged to obſerve, that the buſineſs of Tanjore has been well deliberated by *my Maſters*, has been by them condemned, and their orders in conſequence were not delivered to me, till after they had been laid before his Majeſty's Miniſters for their approval *.

Let me entreat your Highneſs to call to your remembrance, the difficulties you were able to encounter, when your friends power was united to

* This *pretended approval* was *ſurreptitiouſly obtained,* upon a ſtate of facts, which thoſe who procured the orders *knew* to be FALSE. This *impoſition* upon the Secretary of State, is expoſed in the *Obſervations* annexed to theſe Papers.

your

your own.—Remember that union was in the cause of justice, and in *that* cause only can they *be* united. What consequences may attend *even the appearance* of a dis-union?

My Masters gave you their support, when you were alike destitute of money and of power; they will continue their support to you, but the *public faith is pledged* to the Raja of Tanjore †, as well as to your Highness; and the orders to me are, "That the country of Tanjore shall be again "put into the possession of the Raja."

What words shall I use to induce your Highness to make this your *own act*, if all the arguments I have been able to suggest have not had their proper force; and with what an aching heart, after acting in concert with you through so many difficulties, shall I now carry the Company's orders into effect by *their* authority *alone?* The world will justify me in the obedience I shew to the command of my Masters; and having never failed in the part of friendship, in *respect*, and in *propriety* of *behaviour towards you* *, I trust I shall now stand excused, after the pressing manner I have so often urged your Highness to do that what is right and proper, as well respecting your interest as your dignity.

I have the honour to be,
Your Highness's most obedient,
and most humble servant,

Fort St. George,
22d March 1776.

(Signed) PIGOT.

The following is a full and spirited answer to the above letter from Lord Pigot.

† He alludes to the treaty which he himself made with *Pertaub Sing* in the year 1762. The treaty was *forced* upon the Nabob, as appears from his letter to Mr. Pigot of July 17th 1762; besides, the treaty terminated with the life of *Pertaub Sing*; and it had been broken by him, in all its articles.

* For the truth of this assertion, the conferences printed in this collection are recommended to the perusal of the reader.

Tranſlation of a Letter from his Highneſs the Nabob to Lord Pigot, dated 4th Sapher 1190 Hegira, or 25th March 1776.

I Have, on the 25th inſtant, received your Lordſhip's letter, dated the 22d March, and underſtand the contents thereof.—Your Lordſhip writes me, "that after having paid the moſt reſpectful attention to every "argument I have been pleaſed to enforce, you find yourſelf obliged to "obſerve, that the buſineſs of Tanjore has been well deliberated by your "Maſters, has been by them condemned, and their orders, in conſequence, "were not delivered to you, till after they had been laid before his Majeſ-"ty's Miniſters for their approval."

I have already wrote you, in my letter of the 22d January, or 29th Zecaud, the bad conduct of Tuljagee; his requiring aſſiſtance from the Morattas and Hyder Aly Cawn; his ſelling the countries of Tanjore to the Dutch and others, in order to obtain their aſſiſtance in deſtroying the Carnatic and my rights. This letter the Gentlemen of the Company have not yet received, nor have they been informed that the countries of Tanjore, belonging to the Carnatic, were ſold by Tuljagee to the Dutch, which he had no right to do; then how could they give orders on this ſubject? Were they (after they were well informed on this ſubject) to aſk my opinion, as I am their old friend, and have a knowledge of thoſe affairs, and have a right in them, I would agree that they decided juſtly in this buſineſs; but this is not the caſe. When the Gentlemen of the Company, who have their repreſentatives in this country, are not informed of the ſtate of affairs here, how can I imagine that their orders have been approved of by the King's Miniſters? In regard to the order which your lordſhip enforces, I have written to your employers, who are my friends, and have left this buſineſs to their juſtice and enquiry, and wiſh (through your favour) that you may not obſtruct my management in the Tanjore country, till you receive freſh orders. The revenues of that country are laid aſide for the payment of my creditors, who lent their money for that buſineſs.

Your Lordſhip ſays, "Let me intreat your Highneſs to call to your re-"membrance the difficulties you were able to encounter, when your friend's "power was united to your own; remember that union was in the cauſe of "juſtice,

" justice, and in *that* cause only can they be united. What consequences " must attend *even the appearance* of a disunion ?"

I very well remember, that in the time of trouble my father assisted the Company; and from the beginning of my connection with them and the English nation, I have been their invariable friend, in adversity as well as in prosperity, and have been joined in alliance with them ; and I am happy in the recollection of it. It is indeed very true, that my friends the Company justly remembered my former friendship, and gave me their assistance, through their great favour to me; and by the blessing of God, as long as I live and my posterity remains, we will assist my best friends the Company, and we will not forget our obligations to them. I am deeply impressed with the friendship of the Company and the English nation, and my heart is so much affected by it, and the hope of its continuance in future, that I cannot express what I should feel from an appearance of its diminution. From the beginning my friendship with the Company and the Nation, and theirs to me, has been so firmly established and known to the world, that it can never be dissolved.

Your Lordship says,—" My Masters gave you their support, when you " were alike destitute of money and of power; they will continue their sup- " port to you, but the public faith is pledged to the Raja of Tanjore, as " well as to your Highness; and the orders to me are, that the country of " Tanjore shall be put into the possession of the Raja."

It is very true, that when my treasury and power were *expended in the assistance of my friends the Company*, they gave me their assistance, for which I and my sons are obliged to them. I have firm hope that they will continue it to me for ever, for they have strongly promised it to me in their letters; and I place my dependence on the royal letters and promises of his Majesty, and upon his having *included me in the Treaties with the other crowned heads*. I depend upon the letters of the Ministers, who have written to me in the strongest terms on the part of his Majesty. I have already explained to your Lordship in my letter of the 22d January, how far the public faith was concerned in regard to Pertaub Sing, who broke it in his lifetime. Tuljagee likewise broke it, though I have proved that he was *not* concerned in it. I have also in the first paragraph of that letter given an answer in re-

gard

gard to the order of your employers, wherein they desire the country of Tanjore to be given up to Tuljagee.

Your Lordship says, "What words shall I use to induce your Highness to "make this your *own Act*, if all the Arguments I have been able to suggest have not their proper force; and with what an aching heart, after "having acted in concert with you through so many difficulties, shall I now "carry the Company's order into effect by their authority alone?"

I can scarcely say any thing further to your Lordship, having already set forth all the difficulty, loss, and disgrace to me, which will attend your carrying into execution this business in regard to Tanjore; and have begged, *in the name of the King, the Parliament, and the Nation*, that your Lordship would delay it, till you have the fresh orders of the Company; therefore am at a loss to express to your Lordship what pain my heart feels, nor can I explain (in the manner that I ought) what I suffer.

Your Lordship says, "The world will justify me in the obedience I shew "to the orders of my Masters; and having never failed in the part of "friendship, in respect, and in propriety of behaviour towards you, I trust "I shall now stand excused, after the pressing manner I have so often urged "your Highness to do that which is right and proper, as well respecting "your interest as your dignity."

Seeing the justice of the English nation, I hope that you will not act contrary thereto, and destroy the *rights* of the *old* and *firm friend* to the Company, and not hurt the honour of *the Ally of the King of Great Britain*.

I am sure, that in securing my honour and my rights, which is just the same as securing the honour of the King of Great Britain and the English nation, you will be clear in the eyes of his Majesty, *who is my protector*, the Parliament, the Company, and the English nation.

As it is well known to the powers of India, that his Majesty and the Company have promised me their support for ever, it will be for your honour, that you secure this reputation in the eyes of those powers; I firmly trust, that you will shew me favour in supporting my honour, and that you will ſhew friendſhip and good treatment to the invariable friend of the Engliſh nation.

On the 26th of March, Lord Pigot came to the Nabob, about ten of the clock in the morning; and wrote the following paper, with his own hand, and delivered it to his Highneſs, in the preſence of his five ſons.

AS I am now going to Tanjore, I hope the Nabob will let the little time there is, be employed, in conſidering which way I can execute the Company's orders, the moſt to his ſatisfaction; and that when I come away from Tanjore, he will be ſo good as to let Nagif Cawn accompany me, as a guard; it will have a good appearance in the eyes of the world, and ſhew the faith and confidence Lord Pigot has in the Nabob's officers and troops."

Lord Pigot, the day after, ſent to his Highneſs the following letter.

Copy of a Letter from Lord Pigot to the Nabob, dated 27th March 1776.

To the Nabob.

May it pleaſe your Highneſs, *Fort St. George, 27th March 1776.*

THE honour I have in acknowledging the receipt of your letter of the 25th, gives me another opportunity of expreſſing my deſire to execute the orders of the Company, as conformably to your Highneſs's wiſhes, as the faith of my nation and my duty to my employers will admit.

I am, with the greateſt reſpect and eſteem,
Your Highneſs's moſt obliged,
and moſt obedient humble ſervant,

(Signed) PIGOT.

The Nabob, perceiving that Lord Pigot was reſolved to carry into execution the orders with reſpect to Tanjore, made the offers contained in the following letter, as his laſt effort to ſave his rights.

Tranflation of a Letter from his Highnefs the Nabob to Lord Pigot, dated 7th Saphur 1190 Hegira, or 28th March 1776.

I Have received your Lordfhip's letter, dated 27th inftant or 6th Saphur. I have already explained this bufinefs to your Lordfhip, by every means in my power, and I now again requeft, that I may not be *obliged* to give up my rights. Confidering my dependence on the nation, and the Gentlemen of the Company, who are your mafters and my beft friends, I will (after difcharging the debts which I contracted on account of the Tanjore country, and deducting the expences I have been at on account of that country, and the Englifh garrifon which I received into the Fort) *keep the revenues in my poffeffion, without expending one fhilling of them, till the further order of the Company arrives.* The difference between your Lordfhip's intentions and mine is this, your Lordfhip wifhes to do this bufinefs by *force*, and without my *confent*, and I want to *delay* it, till the Company's letter arrives from England. Do me the favour to attend to this reprefentation of your old friend.

Lord Pigot, defpairing to induce the Nabob to relinquifh his *rights*, left Madras on the 29th of March, to execute his defign of reftoring the Raja, in perfon. Having arrived at Cuddalore, and being pleafed with the conveniences, which the Nabob had ordered to be provided for him at every ftage, he wrote to him the following letter.

Copy of a Letter from Lord Pigot to the Nabob, dated 4th April 1776.

To the Nabob.

May it pleafe your Highnefs,

I Will not offend with writing upon bufinefs, but I cannot avoid thanking you for your great attention in writing to your Hamildars and fervants, who have fupplied me upon the road with every thing neceffary. I am now at Cuddalore, and fhall proceed on my journey in the afternoon.

I am, with great efteem,
Your Highnefs's
moft obedient humble fervant,

Cuddalore,
4th April, 1776.

(Signed) PIGOT.

The Nabob anſwered his Lordſhip's *polite* letter, in the following manner.

Tranſlation of a Letter from his Highneſs the Nabob to Lord Pigot, dated 19th Saphur 1190 Hegira, or 9th April 1776.

I Have received your Lordſhip's letter, dated 4th inſtant, wherein you mention that you will not trouble me with matters of buſineſs, but you cannot omit thanking me for the great attention that has been paid you by my Hamildars; and that you leave Cuddalore that evening, with intention to proceed to Tanjore.

I am an old friend to the Company and to you, and think without doubt that your Lordſhip will neither ſay nor do any thing that will give me pain. I wrote to my ſervants to prepare every thing that might be neceſſary to your Lordſhip, and it was my duty to do ſo. The thanks which your Lordſhip expreſſes are returned on my part for your thinking yourſelf obliged.—But I ſhould have been glad if your Lordſhip had *returned to me*, from Cuddalore, inſtead of proceeding from thence.

On the 6th of April, Lord Pigot arrived before Tanjore. He encamped, for the night, on the glacis of the Fort; and, in the morning, went privately to wait upon the Raja. He went, afterwards, in ſtate, with his whole ſuite; and as the Raja (having declared, that had he the treaſures of the Mogul empire his *friend* deſerved them all) complained of the want of money, his Lordſhip told him, that he had brought all the moneyed men in the Company's diſtricts to ſee him. This was a genteel method of ſuggeſting a *loan* to an *unfortunate* prince, who had declared, ſome weeks before, he had only *twelve lacks* in reſerve, and his family jewels. The ſum was ſmall; but the ſtones were valuable. Notwithſtanding the *poverty* of Tuljagee, his Lordſhip was not wanting in paying him the reſpect due to his rank. He viſited him twice every day; yet the ceremony of the Reſtoration did not come on till the 11th of April, though his Lordſhip had arrived on the 6th. The intermediate time was filled up with *private* conferences, for the *ſervice* of the Company. During this week of ſuſpence, the Nabob reminded his Lordſhip in the following letter, of ſome late promiſes he had made.

 Tranſlation

Tranſlation of a Letter from his Highneſs the Nabob to Lord Pigot, dated 10th April 1776, or 10th Saphur 1190 Hegira.

YOUR Lordſhip very well knows, that when it was agreed that the Company's garriſon ſhould be employed in taking care of the Fort of Tanjore, and that a number of my troops ſhould remain there, with Nagif Cawn at their head, as Killidar, your Lordſhip and I were concerned, that the troops there were ſo much in arrrear, as we apprehended that they might mutiny. Your Lordſhip then made me *ſtrong promiſes*, that you would not impede their receiving their pay out of the revenues of the country, according to the Tunkas I had given them; and you likewiſe *aſſured me*, that a thouſand of my Sepoys ſhould remain in the Fort, under the command of Nagif Cawn, and deſired that I would withdraw the others; and it was then determined between you and me, that they ſhould be cantoned at Cumboconum, and receive their pay, according to the orders I had given, on the revenues of that country. In conſequence of this, I wrote to Nagif Cawn, ordering him to give aſſurances to the troops that they ſhould receive their pay out of the revenues of the Tanjore country. This order I ſhewed to your Lordſhip, and you approved of it, and ſent it incloſed in your letter to Colonel Harper, to be delivered by him to Nagif Cawn, who accordingly received it from the Colonel. Nagif Cawn is therefore bound to pay the troops; and I have a great reliance on your Lordſhip to ſhew me favour in this buſineſs, according to *your promiſe*, that I may be clear of any demands on me from the troops.

The following proclamation is a matter of curioſity. Lord Pigot founds the reſtoration of the Raja, on a treaty *forced* by himſelf, or the Nabob, in 1762; as appears from the Nabob's letter of the 17th of July 1762. The treaty was to continue in force, *only* during the life of *Pertaub Sing*; his Lordſhip's *very good friend*. But his Lordſhip makes it here to ſuperſede not only the poſterior orders of the Company, and the repeated annulments of the treaty itſelf, but even the national guarantee, entered into by his Majeſty, and approved by Parliament.

Tanjore

Tanjore, 11th April 1776.

IT is the right honourable Lord Pigot's orders, that the following proclamation, this day made public on the reſtoration of the Raja to the Muſnuk, be read at the head of each corps, and explained to the Seapoys of the different battalions at 7 o'clock.

By order,

(Signed) ROBERT WOOD, Aid de Camp.

The right honourable Lord Pigot, Preſident of the Council for affairs of the Eaſt India Company on the coaſt of Choromandel, and governor of Fort St. George, &c. To all whom it may concern:

"Whereas a treaty was concluded in 1762, between the Nabob of the Carnatic, and the Raja of Tanjore, to which treaty, *the Engliſh* became *guarantee*; and whereas, in *direct violation of the above treaty*, the *troops* of the Eaſt India Company, at the *inſtigation* of the *ſaid Nabob*, did remove the Raja from his government; the Eaſt India Company diſapproving the conduct of their ſervants, have thought proper to require, that the Raja be again reſtored; and in virtue of the orders of the ſaid Company, all officers civil and military, and all perſons under the protection of the ſaid Company, are hereby required to conſider the Raja of Tanjore as again reſtored to the government of his country in the full extent of that government, *as at the concluſion of the treaty of* 1762, and to give him all proper aid and aſſiſtance; dated in Tanjore, this 11th day of April 1776.

(Signed) PIGOT."

The Raja made his appearance a quarter before three in the afternoon; on his appearance on the parade, he was ſaluted with 21 guns, and then was carried round the capital ſtreets, accompanied by the troops of cavalry, the grenadier company of Europeans, the artillery two guns, and ſix companies of grenadier Seapoys, his Lordſhip, &c. and on the Raja's return, he went round the ſquare, was ſaluted by all the officers as he went round; on his going in into the palace, a ſecond ſalute and three volleys of ſmall arms by whole troops; and at 8 o'clock at night, the Raja, in company with his Lordſhip,

‡

ſhip, Meſſ. Dalrymple, Jourdan, Benfield, and Chambers, Colonel Harper, captains Wood and Thomſon, ſat at the couchery, and read the above proclamation in Maratty language, in the preſence of all the Madras merchants and the people of that place; and then all the Madras merchants went with his Lordſhip, Namid Moodu-Kiſtnah, Chippermall Chitty, Chocapah Chitty, Sunca Ramy Chitty, Arnachitte Chitty, Ganduvady Suly Chitty, Bugavan Puntaloo, and Ballur Moodu Chitty, and alſo Sree Salupudy and Irſhippah Chitty of Cuddalore, merchants; they all paid their reſpects to the Raja, with the uſual Nazir of a few pagodas and few gold mohurs, and received Beetle-nut and Roſewater as cuſtomary: Thus ended the ceremony. It was remarked, that the day of Tuljagee's reſtoration was one of the hotteſt in the ſeaſon; yet Lord Pigot, in full dreſs, was carried, without a hat, in an uncovered Palanqueen; ſuch was his zeal for the ſervice!

Though Lord Pigot ſpent many days at Tanjore after the Raja's reſtoration, we do not find him employed in any very important buſineſs. He ordered, it is true, one Cummerow, a man of large property, to be *chabucked*, or whipped on the public parade, for going to viſit the Raja without previouſly aſking his permiſſion; and he commanded, that a poor ſhipwrecked Dutch pedlar, ſhould be bound, on his horſe, with his face towards the tail; and ſo to be driven out of the town, for preſuming to enter it, without his Lordſhip's leave. During theſe acts of *ſummary juſtice*, he wrote the following letter to the Nabob.

Copy of a letter from Lord Pigot to his Highneſs the Nabob, dated 20th April 1776.

May it pleaſe your Highneſs,

I Have had the honour to receive your two letters of 10th April. It would have given me great pleaſure, if you had condeſcended to attend to my advice when I was at Madraſs, as it would have made my journey to theſe parts unneceſſary. Be aſſured, Sir, that I will do every thing in my power to protect your rights, and that I will never interfere in *your buſineſs*, as you are pleaſed to expreſs yourſelf, but when that *buſineſs* is connected with the intereſt of my employers; in ſuch caſe, you may be aſſured, that ſhall always act as appears to me proper, and as you are their old friend and ally, I dare ſay you will approve of my making uſe of your authority.

When I took my leave of you, I acquainted you I was going to Tanjore to replace the Raja in his government, and put him in poſſeſſion of his country by the authority and expreſs commands of the Company. I am ſorry to obſerve to you, that I found, as I paſſed through the country, the proper officers, with all the accounts, had been removed, by your orders, from every village; and I was ſoon informed, that every part of the country was in the ſame ſituation. Every means had been taken to throw difficulties in my way in the execution of the Company's orders, and to diſtreſs the country and inhabitants. In this ſituation, Sir, I thought it the propereſt method to eſcort the Dobeer hither by the Company's troop of cavalry. He is now here, and having been at the head of the revenue department, formerly in the ſervice of the Raja, and lately in yours, if you will pleaſe to order the different Amildars and other officers to return to me with their accounts, juſtice may be done to every man, and the country reſtored in that proper and equitable manner which the world will expect from a friend and old ally of the Company.

It is very true, Sir, that I, as well as every friend you have, and every friend and well-wiſher to the proſperity of the Company, were, are, and muſt continue to be alarmed at the great arrears of pay due to your troops. Perhaps, Sir, it might be made appear, that as much money has been collected from the Tanjore country ſince you were acquainted with the Company's orders *, as would have paid the troops of Najib Cawn, and gone a great way towards diſcharging the arrears due to the reſt. If you turn back to the letters which have been wrote to you, you will find that it was expreſsly inſiſted upon, that an Engliſh garriſon ſhould be put into Tanjore and the Raja ſet at liberty, *without any terms* †; terms would have been diſgraceful on that occaſion.

I always thought that you and your managers had great merit in being able to remove a body of troops to whom ſuch large arrears were due, but I

* This is a miſtake or miſrepreſentation, as will appear from the Nabob's anſwer.

† The reader is requeſted to look back to the Nabob's letter of the 10th of April. It ſeems his Lordſhip's promiſes were verbal, and therefore not *binding*.

never

never made you any promises *on the part of the Company* *; you know well, they had directed the country to be restored to the Raja.

There was one method, and but one which ever occurred to me, likely to relieve you from that burdensome debt due to your troops. I repeatedly told you of it, and I will do so now. It was, that if you would consent to the disbanding these troops, or to the Company's enlisting into their service such of them as I might chuse to accept of, I would use my *endeavours with the Raja of Tanjore* † to suffer a part of the revenues of his country to be applied to the purpose of paying off their arrears; but as this is what you would not hearken to, I see not at present how the Company can be of any service to you upon the occasion. I tell you again and again, that troops *ill-paid will always be the masters of the man who employs them.* Those you have, if they do not disband themselves, which I understand some of them have done, must be disbanded by your Highness, or you will be more and more distressed.

I have the honour to be

your Highness's most obedient humble servant,

Tanjore,
20th April 1776.

(Signed) PIGOT.

Lord Pigot, having *whipt* Cummero, and *bound* the Dutchman on his horse, with his face towards the tail, applied himself to other affairs of no less importance. He ordered *hostile incursions* to be made into the Nabob's other countries, to seize his subjects by *force of arms*, and to bring them prisoners to Tanjore. The news of these outrages arriving at Madras, the Nabob addressed the following letter to the Council.

* But his Lordship made promises on his *own part*.

† It is pity his Lordship has not called Tuljagee *King* of Tanjore. He had the authority of *his Masters* for that appellation; while, at the same time, they divested the Nabob of Arcot, in their instructions to his Lordship, of the title of Highness bestowed upon him by *their own Master*, the King of Great Britain. They call the Nabob only *his Excellency*, an appellation usurped by every petty Polygar.

Translation

Translation of a Letter from his Highness the Nabob, to the President, Governor and Council of Madras, dated 21st April 1776, or 2d Rabbelowell 1190 Hegira.

IN the *fulness of my heart* I now write to you!—I understand, by a letter from the Hamildar of Arrialore, that sixty European horse belonging to the Company, commanded by their officers, together with some of the Company's Sepoys, came from Tanjore, and having crossed the Covey and Colleroon rivers, suddenly entered Arrialore, which is *in my country*, and in the district of Trichinopoly; they surrounded the house of Dubeer and Butchenna, and others *my servants*, turned out by *force* my guard, and in their place put an European one. They then carried away by *force of arms*, as they would prisoners from an enemy's country, my people, together with my papers to Lord Pigot to Tanjore *. The coming of those troops, which are his Lordship's *body guard*, into my country in a *hostile manner*, and carrying away my people and my papers, which are my most sacred property, by *force*; contrary to the friendship, faith and honour of the Company, who are protectors of my honour and dignity in my dominions, is contrary to the *Guarantee* of the English nation to me, and a violation of the alliance of the King of Great Britain with me. Such a violent proceeding has not only destroyed the peace of my country and my authority as Sovereign, but has also been prejudicial to the honour of the whole English nation.—My subjects are all *astonished!* and such confusion has been thrown into my affairs, as Prince of this country, as I cannot possibly explain. I cannot now know what is my right, or what is not; nor in what I have or have not authority; nor how I can give the people of my country support! You, Gentlemen, very well know, that I am unacquainted with the extent of Lord Pigot's powers in this business; but I trust, that my friends, the English, will support my authority in my rights, as a Sovereign, as an ally to the King, and a firm friend to the Company; and that they will satisfy me in their justice.

* This is the outrage which the Supreme Council at Bengal say, in their letter of May 15th to the Presidency of Madras, *requires explanation*; as being "a violation of the independent "rights of the Nabob of the Carnatic; in which character Mahommed Ali Cawn is acknow- "ledged by the treaty of Paris, and is not warranted by the Company's orders."

I am ſo afflicted in my heart, that I am not able to ſay any thing more to you on this ſubject.

The outrage complained of in the preceding letter, is more particularly ſpecified in the following.

Tranſlation of a Letter from Conarirow Hamildar of Arrialore belonging to the Subah of Trichinopoly, to his Highneſs the Nabob, dated 23d Sheeffre 1190 Hegira, or 13th April 1776, received 17th April.

ON this day, being the 23d Sheeffre, about twelve o'clock at noon, there ſuddenly came here from Tanjore, ſixty European horſe belonging to the Company. Narrow Pundet Dubier and Butchana, ſervants to the Circar, were here. The Europeans rode up to the door of the houſe in which they were and diſmounted. The commanding officer, a Deebah and a Brahmin went into the houſe, where the Deebier and Butchana were, and *God knows what they ſaid.* The commanding officer ſome time after came out of the houſe, and obliged to come out the Sepoys of the Circar, who were with the Deebier as a guard, and placed an European guard on the houſe. No one was permitted to go in or out; and it is reported, that as ſoon as it was night, the European horſe went off for Tanjore, and carried priſoners with them, the Deebier and Butchana, together with their papers. I will inform your Highneſs of what may further happen.

The following is the copy of a letter from Lord Pigot, to Major Martinz, who commanded the Nabob's troops at Tanjore, before that place was given up to the Raja.

Major Martinz.

SIR, *Tanjore, 21ſt April 1776.*

I Received from Captain M'Kenzie, a letter of the 15th, incloſing a repreſentation which you had made to him; and I anſwered his letter in ſuch a manner, as I thought would have prevented any inconvenience of the kind you mentioned. This letter muſt have miſcarried; I therefore ſend him another copy, and I have directed him to releaſe your people. Your own prudence will ſhew you, how difficult it will be to prevent diſputes ariſing, arrising, whilst any of the troops of the Nabob remain in parts of the Tanjore country, where the Raja's servants are protected by the Company, in the collection of the Revenues; as such disputes would doubtless give the Nabob much uneasiness. You will therefore please to consider *this* as *sufficient authority* to remove without the limits of Tanjore. I am,

SIR,

Your most obedient humble servant,

(A Copy.) PIGOT.

Major Martinz, Commandant for the Nabob at Tanjore, had sent the following spirited paper to Lord Pigot.

Translation of a Paper sent by Major Martinz.

AS your Lordship has not brought any order from my master for me to give up my power and an account of the revenues of this country to your Lordship, I cannot obey your Lordship's orders; but I, as well as all the world, know that there is great friendship between the East India Company and my Master; therefore I cannot oppose your Lordship. I know very well that the Nabob my Master would be displeased if I conducted myself improperly towards the Company's people, and it is always his order to his servants to consider his honour and the Company as the same. His servants, therefore, strictly attend to this order. If any thing should happen contrary to the interest of my Master, your Lordship is answerable; and I declare publickly, in his name, that it is contrary to justice, and the intention of his Majesty the King of Great Britain, who is Protector to my Master, and contrary to the intention of Parliament and the English nation, that your Lordship is going to *oppress him.*

Major Martinz, Commandant for the Nabob in Tanjore, wrote from Amma Chattram the following answer to Lord Pigot's Letter of the 21st April.

Copy of a Letter from Major Martinz to Lord Pigot, dated 22d April 1776.

The Right Honourable Lord George Pigot.

May it pleafe your Lordfhip,

I Acknowledge the honour of your Lordfhip's letter to me, and I am glad to find that your Lordfhip has taken into confideration the *unjuft* confinement of the Subadar.

Your Lordfhip has been pleafed to order, that I fhould move without the limits of Tanjore, as it would be difficult to prevent difputes arifing whilft any of the Nabob's troops remain in any part of the Tanjore country, where the Raja's fervants are protected by thofe of the Company in the collection of the revenues.

I beg leave to reprefent to your Lordfhip, that at the time I was ordered to march out of Tanjore, a garrifon was then under my command, confifting of about five thoufand men, who were many months in arrears of pay. His Highnefs the Nabob wrote to me, that the whole fhould, without the leaft doubt, be paid at Combaconum, and that your Lordfhip had *agreed to the fame* *; in confequence of which, as likewife by a prudent method, the garrifon marched out; and now I find myfelf much difappointed, and in a very difagreeable fituation.

In a letter which the Nabob wrote to me, dated the 31ft of March, I am acquainted that after your Lordfhip's arrival at Tanjore, and all the country matters were fettled, the troops under my command, difperfed about the country, were to join me at this place, in order that the whole might be paid off, *your Lordfhip having fo promifed*; and that I was to remain here until further orders: therefore fhould I march from hence without orders, fuppofing that the troops would accompany me, (which I doubt much without firft being paid off) though authorifed by your Lordfhip, I might be blamed by the Nabob, and perhaps my commiffion taken from me. I will

* There was fome *Jefuitry* in this affair. A promife was made, but as it was made by *Lord Pigot* and ***not*** by the *Prefident* of Madras, it was evaded; befides, the promife was merely *verbal*, and *therefore* not *binding*.

 immediately

immediately acquaint his Highneſs the Nabob; until ſuch time that I am able to get an anſwer, beg leave to remain; likewiſe it will be ſome few days before all my people come in from the different parts of the country to join me.

I muſt further beg leave to repreſent to your Lordſhip, that from the time that each province or each village was put into the reſtored Raja's poſſeſſion by the protection of the honourable Company's forces, not a man belonging to his Highneſs the Nabob has *oppoſed*, *prevented*, or *interfered*, in the collecting of the revenues, or the ſettling of the country matters.

The protection of the honourable Company to the reſtored Raja, cannot exceed that to his Highneſs, as every one is well convinced of the alliance and friendſhip that has and will exiſt between them.

As the Nabob wrote to me that the troops under my command ſhould be paid off before I ſhould be ordered to march, it being your Lordſhip's intentions, I beg to know, and have to requeſt of your Lordſhip, what meaſures are to be taken on this head. I had an order on this country for the payment of the troops, but the change of government has put an entire ſtop to its being paid.

Myſelf, as well as other European officers, have been at the *expence of building** and repairing quarters, when in the garriſon of Tanjore, the liſt of which was ſent to his Highneſs the Nabob, amounting to 7000 pagodas, who has been pleaſed to ſend up an order on this country for its payment, but it has likewiſe been put a ſtop to.

I ſhould not trouble your Lordſhip with ſuch a long epiſtle, but knowing your Lordſhip's good inclinations towards giving juſtice to every individual, has been the reaſon of my being ſo bold; and ſo far from thinking your Lordſhip

* Many of thoſe officers were forced to remove from houſes, *their own property*, by the violence of his Lordſhip; particularly Mr. Salmon paymaſter for the Nabob at Tanjore, though lying in bed of a dangerous illneſs, was turned out of a houſe he himſelf had built.

will

will take it amiſs of me, that I hope, and make no doubt, but that it will meet with your Lordſhip's approbation.

I have the honour to be
with the greateſt reſpect,
My Lord,
Your Lordſhip's moſt obedient,
and moſt humble ſervant,
(Signed)

Amma Chattram,
April 22d, 1776.

The Nabob complains, in the following letter, of the *hoſtile* incurſions made into the territories of the Carnatic, by Lord Pigot's orders; under the *falſe* pretence of the diſtricts invaded being a part of the province of Tanjore.

*Tranſlation of a Letter from his Highneſs the Nabob to Mr. Stratton *. Dated April 27th 1776, or 8th Rabelowell 1190 Hegira.*

I Have, in my letter of the 2d Rabelowell, explained to you my uneaſineſs of mind; I am now informed that the Company's Sepoys are marched to take poſſeſſion of ſome diſtricts of Ramnade and Shevagunga, on the *groundleſs repreſentations* of Tuljagee, who ſays that they *belong to Tanjore.* The countries of Ramnade and Shevagunga never depended on Tanjore, but were diſtinct countries; but ſome time ſince, in the government of Mr. Du Pre, Tuljagee (preſuming on his power) took poſſeſſion of ſome diſtricts of thoſe countries, for which he was puniſhed; and he gave it under his hand, that he would not in future take any ſuch liberties: therefore I am now very much ſurpriſed, that the Company's people ſhould march into thoſe countries on the falſe repreſentations of Tuljagee. Before Lord Pigot ſet out for Tanjore, I ſent orders to the Hamildars in that country not to oppoſe any one ſent by his Lordſhip. Though my people were very numerous, they gave no oppoſition, even to ſingle guards of the Company's Sepoys ſent by his Lordſhip, though they treated them worſe than *enemies* would have done, and put my principal people in priſon, who quietly ſubmitted to it. The countries of Ramnade and Shevagunga by no means depend upon Tanjore, as is known to every one; therefore I ſent no orders to my Hamildars in

* The acting governor, during Lord's Pigot's abſence from Madras.

Ramnade. I therefore requeſt that you will inform me what orders I am to ſend to my Hamildars there, in this buſineſs.

Nigif Cawn, the Nabob's military governor at Tanjore, wrote the following ſenſible letter to his Maſter, concerning the hoſtilities committed by Lord Pigot. He informs him by report, that the outrages complained of in the preceding letter were intended by his Lordſhip.

Tranſlation of a Letter from Nigif Cawn to his Highneſs the Nabob. Dated 25th Saphur, Monday 15th April 1776.

AFTER a great deal of trouble, I could not obtain more than a hundred and ninety bullocks, and I very much wanted to go to Arrialore. Theſe bullocks I divided amongſt your Highneſs's ſervants, by giving to each of them one or two. This day the Company's troopers who went to Arrialore, returned, and brought with them, by *force*, the Debir, Bachannah, &c. and others of your Highneſs's ſervants to Tanjore. Lord Pigot is gone to Vellum, and laſt night the Killedar there wrote to me to know what he was to do. I wrote him in anſwer, that we were ſo ſituated that matters were carried on by *force*, and ſhould he be *turned out by force*, he ſhould go with his people to Arrialore. People ſay that Lord Pigot wants to take Chivagunda, Ramanade, and other forts in that neighbourhood by his own power, on which he places great *value*; and it is my opinion that it is not far from his intention. Your Highneſs, therefore, does well, in *ſilently expecting juſtice* from his *Lordſhip's Maſter* * for his violent proceedings. God is your ſupport, and you may expect juſtice without uneaſineſs, from his Lordſhip's *Maſter*, for all will end well. I have not yet heard that Nizam Udein Cawn has left Cumbeconum. The Company's people have got poſſeſſion of the villages in this neighbourhood, and have, no doubt, before this poſſeſſed themſelves of all the country.

The following letter from Major Martinz to the Nabob contains the particulars of the hoſtilities committed by Lord Pigot's orders, at Cambeconum.

* The King of Great Britain.

To

To his Highneſs the Nabob Wallejaw.

May it pleaſe your Highneſs,

I Am ſorry to acquaint your Highneſs, that yeſterday the 14th inſtant, as I was at the Cutchery, with Nizam Mooddein Hummed Cawn, and ſeveral of the horſemen, a company of the Honourable Company's Sepoys, who in the morning arrived at *Combeconum*, and halted at the *Palace-gate*, came about twelve o'clock at noon into the *Cutchery* and ſaid, that it was Lord Pigot's orders delivered to him, by Captain M'Kenzie, that he, the Jemidar, ſhould apprehend the head manager of *Combeconum*, and make him tye the Zorran; and alſo beat the Zom Zom, and publiſh through the town, that henceforth no orders from your Highneſs, or any of your Highneſs's ſervants, were to be obeyed in the country. The manager was at this time in the garden, and whilſt the Jemidar was talking to me, four Sepoys had ſeized upon him, and were pulling him away by force.—We remonſtrated with them, and told them, that we had received no orders from your Highneſs concerning ſuch proceedings; and that we could not give our conſent thereto: To which the Jemidar replied, that ſuch were his orders, and that he muſt comply with them, whether we chooſed or not. We then told him, that all the world knew the friendſhip that ſubſiſted between the Honourable Company and your Highneſs; and that your Highneſs would be very much diſpleaſed, ſhould we offer any violence, offenſive or defenſive to the Honourable Company's ſervants, on this or any other occaſion, and declared that it was a palpable violence done againſt your Highneſs; and that they, the Company's ſervants, were to be anſwerable to your Highneſs, for all the damages that might occur from ſuch proceedings. The Jemidar returned for anſwer, that it did not concern him, but that he muſt comply with his orders; on ſo ſaying, the manager was pulled away by four Sepoys from our preſence. A little while after, the Zoran was tyed, and the above-mentioned publication made through the town.

About half after ſix at night, Captain M'Kenzie with a battalion of the Honourable Company's Sepoys arrived, and with him one Hiſſindrow, a head Renter appointed by the Raja for that diſtrict. The ſaid Captain came to the Cutchery, and told me and Nizam Moodeen Hammed Cawn, that it was Lord Pigot's poſitive orders to him, to march to *Combeconum* with his battalion, to take the ſaid Hiſſindrow, and to ſee him placed and eſtabliſhed head

Head Renter of this diſtrict; and that the Cutchery was to be cleared off for him immediately, and that we might go where we pleaſed.—We told Captain M'Kenzie, that we were placed in our different ſtations by your Highneſs, and that we could by no means willingly conſent to their proceedings. Captain M'Kenzie replied, that ſuch were his Lordſhip's orders, and he was obliged to obey: adding, that we muſt leave the *Cutchery.* We then told him, that we and all the world knew, the friendſhip and alliance that ſubſubſiſted between your Highneſs and the Honourable Company and the Engliſh Nation; and that your Highneſs would be exceedingly diſpleaſed were we to offer any violence, offenſive or defenſive, againſt any of the Honourable Company's ſervants; and that this proceeding was an unjuſt violence againſt your Highneſs, contrary (as we imagined) to the will of his Britannic Majeſty; and that we therefore expected his Lordſhip would be anſwerable to your Highneſs, for any damages that might occur, from our being forced away from our ſtations in this country by his Lordſhip, without your Highneſs's order to us. We then went away from the Cutchery, and the ſaid Hiſſandrow ſat and took poſſeſſion of it, where crowds of the inhabitants aſſembled.

I ſhall do myſelf the honour to acquaint your Highneſs of any thing elſe that may happen. I have the honour to be,

May it pleaſe your Highneſs,
Your Highneſs's moſt obedient, moſt
humble, and moſt faithful ſervant,

Amma Chattram,
April 15, 1775.

(Signed) M. MARTINZ.

The following letter to the Nabob, is on the ſame ſubject.

Tranſlation of a Letter from Nizam Udeen Achmed Cawn at Cambeconum, to his Highneſs the Nabob, dated 24th Souffee, or 14th April 1776.

AT ſeven o'clock this evening, ſome Hircarrahs belonging to Tuljagee came to Papanaſſy, and with them were fifty Sepoys. Upon being aſked who they were, the Sepoys anſwered, that they belonged to the Company, and were come with orders to the Hamildars, for them to deliver up to them the poſſeſſion of the Papanaſſy country. The Hamildar told them, I am the Nabob's ſervant, what buſineſs have I with your orders?

Upon

Upon this the Sepoys ſeized the Hamildar, his Piſhcar and Ameen, and carried them to the Cutchery, where they confined them under a guard. I hear that one battalion of Sepoys and two Guns have marched from the Fort of Tanjore for Cumbeconum, and that they are advanced half the way. I have given notice to all the Hamildars, and now write this for your Highneſs's information.

The writer of the following letter is a foreigner and not maſter of the Engliſh language. Some further hoſtilities committed by Lord Pigot.

Copy of a letter from John Henry Pickard to his Highneſs the Nabob, dated 15th April 1776.

His Highneſs the Nabob Waielaugaiee, &c. &c. &c.

May it pleaſe your Highneſs,

I MAKE bold to acquaint your Highneſs, that the 13th inſtant I was ordered by Major Martinz, to go to Mayavaram, and there to ſtay by the four companies of my battalion, and to be in conjunction with Albrur Cawn Cawnſahil, in caſe the Company's troops were to come and drive us out of the country, that we ſhould by no means make any reſiſtance againſt them. With this orders I arrived here the ſame evening, and this morning at 8 o'clock, one guard and three Arcars came into this place. I ſend my adjutant Zemindar, to aſk them where they come from, and where they was to go to, and whom people they were. They made anſwer to my Zemindar, that they came from Tanjore, and they belong to the Raja, and ſo they went on to the Hamildar houſe; and Cawn Saib here had a guard over the Amuldar of my people, and he had ſend for him ſeveral times, but he did not come; but when thoſe guard from Tanjore, and the Arcars came to him, he then got up and came to Cawn Saib with my guard and the others along with him. Cawn Saib and I, we both aſked the Havildar of the guard and the Arcars whoms people they were, they made anſwer the Raja's, and the Arcars had an open paper in their hands, which they ſhewed to Cawn Saib, but it was for the Amildar from the Raja, wherein he deſires him to keep the rent from this country for him, and not to pay a lack more to your Highneſs. Cawn Saib and I then made anſwer, that we knowed nothing about the Raja of Tanjore, but your Highneſs was our maſter, and the country

country and revenues belonged to your Highneſs, and the ſame Amildar or Renter was yours, ſo that we did not know any thing about the Raja at all, ſo they might go where they pleaſed; as for the Amildar and country they had nothing to do with it. Upon that the Arcars wanted to talk more; Cawn Saib then told them, that he had nothing to do with them, they ſhould go about their buſineſs, if not he would drive them away; upon that the Havildar of the guard ſaid, that they were Company's people, were ſend by Lord Pigot's orders with this Arcars, to take poſſeſſion of this country for the Raja, and they belonged to Captain Mackenzie battalion, and their captain would come to-morrow or next day with the battalion. Cawn Saib and I then told the Havildar, Very well, if you are Company's people, and ſend by Lord Pigot's orders, we will not mattel with you, but that we cannot leave the country without an order from our maſter, and we will immediately write to the Nabob about it, and likewiſe to Major Martinz, and if we do get an order from them, that we ſhall give the country up to you, we then will do it, but before we cannot; and if your captain comes with his battalion and drives us away by force, we then cannot help ourſelves; but muſt go, as the Company and Nabob are in very great alliance together, we muſt ſuffer to be drove away without reſiſtance; but hoping that Lord Pigot, or who comes to drive us away in his name, will be anſwerable to the Nabob for all the loſs and ill-treatment. Upon that the Havildar ſaid nothing for ſome time, after that they wanted to take the Amildar away, out of Cawn Saib's houſe, in order they might go and tye the Turane for the Raja; Cawn Saib then told them again, I have told you before, that this Amildar is in the Nabob's ſervice, and Amildar of this country, and great quantity of accounts in his charge. I therefore cannot let him go with you. If you have orders from your maſter to make force with us here, or to take the Nabob's renters by force, that is indied more than ever is heard of as yet. In the mean time, one Nagues guard more came to join the Havildars guard, and when the two guard got together in Cawn Saib's houſe, the two Amildars were ſitting cloſe by Cawn Saib, when they laid hold of them and pooled both the Amildar away from Cawn Saib, which was 3 o'clock in the afternoon, and ſo they begun to tye new Turns in the Raja name. I humbly beg your Highneſs pleaſes to be ſo kind and ſend me an order what I am to do in this caſe, to be drove away

 out

out of the country by two guards of Sepoys; ſo I beg leave to remain with the greateſt reſpect,

Your Highneſs's
most devoted, moſt dutyful,
moſt obedient and moſt humble ſervant,
JOHN HENRY PICKARD.

Mayararum,
15th April 1776.

The ſame apology with regard to the language muſt be made for the following letter from the ſame officer. More hoſtilities.

Copy of a Letter from John Henry Pickard to the Nabob, dated 16th April 1776.

To his Highneſs the Nabob Waulaujah, &c. &c. &c.

May it pleaſe your Highneſs,

I Have done myſelf the honour yeſterday to acquaint your Highneſs of what has happened here. Now I make bold to lay before your Highneſs's feet, that laſt night one company more of the Company's troops arrived here, and there has been one Amildar, which the two guards yeſterday did not take; but this morning, after that company is came here, they have ſend four guards to his houſe, and brought him priſoner to the Cutchery; and after that, they ſend one guard to Abrai Cawn Cawnſaib's houſe, to take away all the Circar's accounts; and is ſhort, they ſend all round about, to catch all the Sarcars, Muſſadirs, and all the writers, and Abrai Cawn Cawnſaib; he is afraid that they will lay hold upon him very ſoon, if he ſtays here any longer, he therefore has deſired me to march to Amma Chetrum, as ſoon I do get my people together, which I told him that I cannot do, or I cannot leave this place without an order from your Highneſs, or elſe from my commanding officer, Major Martinz. I have likewiſe been informed, that Lord Pigot has ſend the European troop and two companies of Sepoys to Argalore; and they have carried the Dubin priſoner to Tanjore, and this morning one officer and one company of Sepoys is gone by here to Shealy, and Good knows how ſoon they do drive me and my people out of this place, as the Bramineys have this day drove the butcher out of the place, who has been here ever ſince our people have been here. This is the way they do go on with your Highneſs, and that in your Highneſs's own country.

I am

I am indeed at a loss to know your Highness's kind pleasure, I therefore humbly beg your Highness to honour me with your kind orders; so I beg your highness's kind leave to remain with the greatest respect,

Your Highness's
Most devoted, most dutiful, most obedient,
and most humble servant,

Mayararum,
16th April 1776.

JOHN HENRY PICKARD.

The Nabob sent the following answer to Lord Pigot's letter of the 20th of April; a very spirited letter! it overturns his Lordship's arguments, and accuses him of breaches of *verbal* promises.

Translation of a Letter from his Highness the Nabob to Lord Pigot, dated 10th Rabbelowell 1190 Hegira, or 29th April 1776.

YOUR Lordship's letter of the 20th instant, written in the English language, has been presented to me. I am in sorrow; but so much of the meaning as I understand, I will answer.

Your Lordship says, "It would have given me great pleasure, if you had "condescended to attend to my advice when I was at Madras, as it would "have made my journey to these parts unnecessary."

From the beginning of my firm friendship with the Company and the English nation, I have always taken the advice of the deputies of my best friends, as they protected my honour and rights; but when their advice was repugnant to my honour and interest, I then explained to them my situation. Your Lordship well knows, that after your arrival, when I understood the Company's order, which you brought out, relative to that country, I agreed cheerfully to receive the Company's garrison, though I was sensible that the order had been given by the Gentlemen in England, from *their want of information* * in the true state of affairs here. This I always uniformly represented to you, and very earnestly requested your permission to lay before the Company the true state of affairs, and that you would delay interfering in my rights, till the Company had considered this business, and given their answer. Notwithstanding this would not have been of any pre-

* This has been fully and repeatedly explained.

judice

judice to the Company, your Lordſhip would not agree to it, but ſeemed *inclined on going yourſelf to Tanjore* *. I repeatedly told you that a ſingle Peon belonging to the Company would be ſufficient for that buſineſs, becauſe my people had my orders againſt giving any oppoſition to the Company's people, therefore that your going was *unneceſſary* †.

You ſay, " Be aſſured, Sir, that I will do every thing in my power to " protect your rights, and that I will never interfere in *your buſineſs*, as " you are pleaſed to expreſs yourſelf, but when *that buſineſs* is connected " with the intereſt of my employers; in ſuch caſe you may be aſſured that I " will always act as appears to me proper, and as you are their old friend " and ally, I dare ſay that you will approve of my making uſe of *your au-* " *thority*."

I thank you for your good diſpoſition to protect my rights, and not to interfere in *my buſineſs*, and will be more thankful to you if you do ſo in future. From the beginning of the friendſhip between the Company and me, I have with all my authority, on every opportunity, contributed, and ever will contribute, to the intereſt and advantage of the Company, and they (who are my beſt friends) have always conſidered our mutual intereſt. I hope in God that our friendſhip will not be diminiſhed during the lives of me and my poſterity. You yourſelf may judge, if I, who am the *ally of the king of Great Britain*, and the firſt friend of the Company and the Engliſh nation, can approve of my authority being made uſe of in hurting my honour and deſtroying my rights. I never gave my conſent in this buſineſs, but have always uniformly expreſſed my diſapprobation of it, both verbally and in writing, which will appear by my letters of the 22d and 25th January, 3d and 26th February, and 19th, 25th, and 28th March laſt.

Your Lordſhip ſays, " When I took my leave of you, I acquainted you " I was going to Tanjore, to replace the Raja in his government, and to put " him in poſſeſſion of his country, by the authority and expreſs commands of " the Company. I am ſorry to obſerve to you, that I found, as I paſſed " through the country, the proper officers with all the accounts had been

* His Lordſhip had buſineſs of his *own* to tranſact in that place. The Nabob tells him, that a ſingle Peon would have been ſufficient, as nothing but *implicit acquieſcence* was meant.

† His Lordſhip knew better the ſtate of his *own* affairs.

" removed

" removed by your orders from every village; and I was ſoon informed,
" that every part of the country was in the ſame ſituation, every means had
" been taken to throw difficulties in my way in the execution of the Com-
" pany's orders, and to diſtreſs the country and the inhabitants. In this
" ſituation, Sir, I thought it the propereſt method to eſcort the Dabeer hi-
" ther by the Company's troop of cavalry. He is now here, and having
" been at the head of the revenue department formerly in the ſervice of the
" Raja, and lately in yours; if you will pleaſe to order the different Amil-
" dars and other officers to return with their accounts, juſtice may be done
" to every man, and the country reſtored in that proper and equitable man-
" ner which the world will expect from a friend and old ally of the Com-
" pany."

Before your Lordſhip ſet out on your journey, I had ordered the Dabeer and my other ſervants to come to me, and they were come part of the way, and were at Arrialore, which is in the Trichinopoly country. When you reached the Tanjore country, all my principal Amildars, *viz.* Mahommid Abrar Cawn, Nizam Udan Mahommid Cawn, Ali Dil Cawn, &c. who were all my old ſervants, ſome of them for two generations, were there with their accounts, employed in their buſineſs, and received you with the greateſt reſpect. After I gave orders for giving up the care of the fort of Tanjore to the Company, there were in it five or ſix thouſand men. My principal Amildars as above mentioned had my orders not to give any oppoſition to your people; therefore, only *two guards* of *your ſeapoys*, in the face of *a large body* of *my troops*, treated my ſaid Amildars with the greateſt indignity, contempt, and diſgrace, they would not have treated enemies in the ſame manner, having diſgracefully impriſoned them, and taken from them their accounts. They afterwards ſent Drurus round the towers and the country of Tanjore, proclaiming that *no rice ſhould be ſold to my people*, nor any protection given them; that whoever did protect any of my people ſhould be puniſhed and fined; yet this was not ſufficient, but ſixty European horſe paſſed the Coleroon and Cavery rivers, and went to Arrialore which is in the Trichinopoly country. What they did there, my honour and concern will not allow me to dwell upon!—You know it full well!—After all this, I cannot diſcover what difficulties were thrown in your way in the execution of the Company's orders. I never could ſuppoſe that ſuch indignities would be offered to me.—There is ſuch confuſion now thrown into my affairs, that

7 no

no man in my country can place any dependance upon my protection. If your Lordſhip wiſhes to have the accounts of the country, according to the cuſtoms of the country, the accounts of every village are to be found in it.—My ſervants and my papers muſt come to me; now what perſon and what papers do you require of me, as being out of your power? You know beſt, if it is your intention to do juſtice to my creditors and my troops, for I have repeatedly wrote to you and ſpoke to you on this ſubject.

Your Lordſhip ſays, " It is very true, Sir, that I, as well as every friend " you have, and every friend and well-wiſher to the proſperity of the Com- " pany, were, are, and muſt continue to be, alarmed at the great arrears " of pay due to your troops; perhaps, Sir, it might be made appear, that " as much money has been collected from the Tanjore country ſince you " were acquainted with the Company's orders, as would have paid the troops " of Najeeb Cawn, and gone a great way towards diſcharging the arrears due " to the reſt.

" If you look back to the letters which have been wrote to you, you " will find, that it was expreſsly inſiſted upon, that an Engliſh garriſon " ſhould be put into Tanjore, and the Raja ſet at liberty without any " terms. Terms would have been diſgraceful on that occaſion."

There was but one diſtrict of the Tanjore country ſet aſide for the payment of the troops; all the reſt was for the payment of the creditors, as I ſet forth to your Lordſhip. At the time I received the garriſon of my friends into the fort of Tanjore, I and my counſellors were ſure, from your Lordſhip's *fixed manner of ſpeaking*, that you would have continued Najib Cawn Kelledar of the fort; and to be fully convinced of it, I repeatedly mentioned it to your Lordſhip, and was more confirmed in my opinion. As there are now doubts thrown into this buſineſs, perhaps there likewiſe may in your Lordſhip's *promiſe* for the payment of the troops, with which I acquainted Najib Cawn when I wrote him the order to withdraw my troops from the garriſon, and to remain at Cambeconum till paid off. This order Mr. Chambers tranſacted and ſhewed to you; and after you had approved of it, you incloſed it to Colonel Harper to be delivered to Najib Cawn who became ſecurity to the troops that they ſhould be paid; in conſequence of which, they were content and marched to Cambeconum. Had I then imagined

gined that these doubts would have arisen, I would have transacted this business by writing *.

Your Lordship says, " I always thought that you and your managers had
" great merit in being able to remove a body of troops to whom such large
" arrears were due, but I never made you any promises on the part of the
" Company; you know well, they had directed the country to be restored
" to the Raja."

What your Lordship says on this subject appears to me to proceed from your goodness, but it was the order that was approved of by your Lordship and sent to Najib Cawn, that was the cause of taking out the troops; therefore it is you that have the merit in this affair †.

Your Lordship says, " There was one method, and but one, which ever
" occurred to me likely to relieve you from that burdensome debt due to
" your troops; I repeatedly told you of it, and I will do so now. It was,
" that if you would consent to the disbanding those troops, or to the
" Company's enlisting into their service such of them as I might chuse
" to accept of, I would use my endeavours with the Raja of Tanjore, to
" suffer a part of the revenues of this country to be applied to the purpose
" of paying off their arrears: But as this is what you would not hearken to,
" I see not at present how the Company can be of any service to you upon
" the occasion. I tell you again and again, that troops ill paid, will always
" be the masters of the man who employs them; those you have, if they do
" not disband themselves, which I understand some of them have done,
" must be disbanded by your Highness, or you will be more and more
" distressed."

Before your arrival from England, the revenues of my country were conveyed by Tunkas, given by me to my creditors and my troops, as I told your Lordship. The crops upon which the troops depended for their pay, were not ripe; when they were, they hoped to receive it, but my rights were disturbed. You know very well, that my honour will not permit me to receive, as a favour, any thing from my subjects or my servants.—*Such as*

* The promises were *verbal*, and, therefore, *not to be regarded*.

† These arguments *come home* to his Lordship.

Rajas

Rajas I have many amongst my servants.—The Tanjore country *must* be answerable for the demands of my creditors, and my troops on it, and the justice of this I submit to my best friends. You know that always, and on every opportunity, I am the firm friend of the Company, and a *true* and *grateful ally* to the king of Great Britain, and a friend to the whole English nation, and that nothing can diminish my friendship for them.

An answer to his Highness's letter of April 27th, waving the entering upon the subject of it, as Lord Pigot was expected back in a few days.

Copy of a Letter from Mr. Stratton to his Highness the Nabob, dated 30th April 1776.

To his Highness the Nabob, &c. &c.

May it please your Highness,

I Have had the honour to receive your letter, dated the 27th instant, copy of which I immediately transmitted to Lord Pigot, who I expect here in a few days, when I have not a doubt he will clear up every thing to your satisfaction.

I have the honour to be with profound respect,

May it please your Highness,
Your Highness's
most sincere, most obedient, and
most humble servant,
GEORGE STRATTON.

Fort St. George,
30th April 1776.

The following letter proves the exactness with which the Nabob fulfils his engagements to the Company, notwithstanding the injustice and tyranny of the Company towards him.

Translation of a Letter from his Highness the Nabob to George Stratton, Esq. dated April 29th 1776, or 10th Rabbicowell 1190 Hegira.

I Have paid for the Company, for which you will please to send me a receipt, 115,000 pagodas, and acquaint you, that 100,000 of this sum is on on account of the Kist of the districts of Tripassore, &c. due the 31st January last; and 1500 pagodas on account of Poonamallee Kist, from the 1st of January last, to the 30th April 1776.

The following is also on money transactions.

Translation of a Letter from the Nabob to Mr. Stratton, acting Governor of Madras, dated and received the 30th April 1776.

THE current charges of the seven original battalions belonging to my service, kept up by the Company, and of the three additional battalions *I agreed to take* into pay at the time of the Tanjore expedition †, together with extra expences and 2 lacks 65,045 pagodas 45 fan 16 cash for the pay of three battalions of Sepoys, from the 16th August 1770, to the 31st June 1773, which my letter to the Governor and Council of the 25th October 1773, mentions it to be given as a present to the Company, in consideration of the Tanjore expedition, amount in the whole to 871,666 pagodas 24 fan. This sum I have paid into the Company's cash, from the 1st of May 1775, to the 30th April 1776; as follows.

In ready money, on account of the pay of the before-mentioned 10 battalions of Sepoys, one of which is gone to Bombay, three lacks of pagodas (300,000 pagodas), on account of the present to the Company above-recited, pagodas two hundred and sixty-six thousand and forty-five, two fanams and sixteen cash (266,045 2 16), on account of extra charges forty-two thousand six hundred and eighty-five pagodas, twenty-one fanams and sixty-four cash (42,685 21 64). In bills two hundred and sixty-two thousand nine hundred and thirty-six pagodas (262,936). Total in ready money 608,730 24; and in bills 262,936 pagodas, make the sum of 871,666 24 pagodas, the whole amount of my agreement, which, by the blessing of God, I have entirely cleared off; and the expences of the army, on account of both Tanjore expeditions, have been also discharged.

† The keeping up and paying those three additional battalions, were among the conditions, which the Nabob granted to the Company, in consideration of their assistance in taking Tanjore.

It

It used to be a rule with former governors, to send me my accounts every three months, but it is now fifteen months since I received any.—I shall esteem it a favour, if you will send me my accounts, commencing from the date of those you last sent me, and brought down to the 30th of this month. Consider me always as the firm and obliged friend of the Company.

What can I say more?

Mr. Stratton sent the following answer to preceding letters from the Nabob.

Copy of Mr. Stratton's Letter to his Highness the Nabob, dated 3d May 1776.

To his Highness the Nabob, &c. &c.

May it please your Highness,

I Have had the honour to receive your two letters, dated the 29th April, one accompanying a letter for Lord Pigot, which, agreeable to your Highness's request, I forwarded immediately to him. The other letters advises me of your Highness having sent into the Company's cash one hundred and fifteen thousand pagodas; and that one hundred thousand of this sum is on account of the Kist of the districts of Trepassore, &c. due 31st January last; and fifteen thousand pagodas account Poonamallee Kist, from the 1st January last to the 30th April 1776. I have also had the honour to receive your Highness's letter, dated 30th ult. advising me, that you have paid into the Company's cash, from 1st May 1775 to the 30th April 1776, account current charges, &c. as follows, in ready money, on account of the ten battalions of Sepoys, three lacks of pagodas; on account of the pay of three battalions of Sepoys, from 16th August 1770 to 31st June 1773, two hundred and sixty-six thousand and forty-five pagodas, two fanams and sixteen cash, which your letter to the Governor and Council of the 25th October 1773, mentions to be given as a present to the Company, in consideration of the Tanjore expedition, on account of extra charges. Forty-two thousand six hundred and eighty-five pagodas, twenty-one fanams, and sixty-four cash; and in bills, two hundred and sixty-two thousand nine hundred and thirty-six pagodas; making altogether in ready money and bills, eight hundred and seventy-one thousand six hundred and sixty-six pagodas, twenty-four fanams, being the whole amount of your Highness's agreement. In answer to the above I have the honour to acquaint your Highness, that I have received from you as follows;

Two

Two bills on Jasing for — — — —	119,000
In ready money — — — —	78,000
And one bill which accompanied your Highness's last letter on Jasing for — — — — —	143,936

Your Highness's account has due credit for the ready money, as you will have also for the bills when discharged. The above bills and ready money, with the sums your Highness has already paid to Lord Pigot and to Mr. Wynch, amount to eight hundred and seventy-one thousand six hundred and sixty-six pagodas, being the whole of the payments agreed to be made by your Highness from 1st May 1775, to 30th April 1776.—Your Highness has also paid in bills and ready money, the sum of one hundred and fifteen thousand pagodas, being in full for the Kist, due on account of the Trepassore, &c. districts, the 31st January 1776, and on account of the Kists of the Poonamullee country to 30th ult.

I am very much obliged to your Highness for the punctuality you have shewn in the above payments, and your accounts are ordered to be made out to the time your Highness desires.

I have the honour to be with profound respect,

May it please your Highness,

Your Highness's most sincere

most obedient and most humble servant,

Fort St. George,
3d May 1776.

GEORGE STRATTON.

Lord Pigot having returned from Tanjore on the 5th of May, endeavoured to *extort* an approbation of his measures from the Nabob. The following paper, with its title, will speak for itself. It was in this very way that Mr. Pigot *forced* the Nabob to sign the treaty of 1762, which his Lordship makes the basis of the restoration of Tuljagee.

Copy of a Paper written by Lord Pigot with a Pencil, and given by him to his Highness the Nabob of the Carnatic, that his Highness might write the Contents in a Letter to his Lordship. May 11th, 1770.

I AM very happy at my friend's return. I forgive you for every thing you have done *. The man who is faithful to his master will ever be so to his

* His Lordship *owns* that his conduct stood in need of forgiveness.

*

his friend. Now you have finiſhed the Company's buſineſs, I hope you will not forget mine. I will lay before you the whole ſtate of my affairs, and I deſire your aſſiſtance to *ſettle them* to the ſatisfaction of the Company, that I may be happy.

I certify that this is a true Copy of the above-mentioned paper,

JAMES WOOLEY,
Secretary to the Nabob.

Lord Pigot anſwers the letters ſent by his Highneſs to Mr. Stratton, the acting Governor, during his Lordſhip's abſence. The letter is dictated by that reſentment which his Lordſhip entertained againſt the Nabob, for refuſing to write to him the above paper, and conſequently for not approving of his tranſactions at Tanjore.

Copy of a Letter from Lord Pigot to his Highneſs the Nabob, dated 13th May 1776.

To the Nabob.

May it pleaſe your Highneſs,

ON reading over the proceedings of Mr. Stratton, and the other Gentlemen of the Council, I find two letters from you addreſſed to Mr. Stratton, which I ſhall now do myſelf the honour to anſwer.

That your mind is full of trouble and uneaſineſs does not ſurpriſe me; *bad counſellors have often diſtracted a mind as great as your Highneſs's* *.

Your ſon Ameer-ul-Omrah perhaps forgot to inform you, that Naroo Pundet, the Dobbier, after Tanjore was taken, told your ſon he would not deſert his Maſter in his misfortunes, and refuſed to act until he carried him to the Raja, and deſired him to lay his commands upon him. Was it noble, was it generous, was it honourable, was it juſt, to impriſon this venerable old man, between 70 and 80 years of age? This *publick officer*; this firſt officer of the Tanjore revenue; *this officer of the publick*, not your Highneſs's ſervant †.

* This is truly a *home* ſtroke of his Lordſhip!

† Yet he *ſerved* his Highneſs. It is pity, a paragraph poſſeſſing ſuch *eloquence of words*, ſhould contain ſuch groſs *miſrepreſentations of facts*.

From this man * I learnt that your Highneſs had received from the Tanjore country, in the three years you have had it in your poſſeſſion, 40 lacks of pagodas, *which will be a great ſatisfaction to my Employers*, as they will be confident that the expence your Highneſs has been at, could not have amounted to near that ſum.

I learned alſo from the Dobbier, that the revenue of Tanjore, for this year, amounted only to 12 lacks of pagodas, that there remained only three lacks to be collected by the Raja ‡, and that your Highneſs's receipts, orders, and the uſual charge, amounted to full nine. *This* was *a great ſatisfaction to me*, as I truſt it will enable your Highneſs to pay the arrears due to your troops. The good purpoſes the meaſure has anſwered, will, I hope, appear to you a ſufficient reaſon for eſcorting || the Dobbier to Tanjore.

Shall the gates of Arrialore, or any other gates in the Pauyen-Ghaut §§ be ſhut againſt the troops of the Company, who have fought for you near 30 years, when they aſk admittance by my authority; I hope not. This would be an improper return to the man who put your Highneſs in poſſeſſion of them, upon your ſolemn aſſurances that there was no diſtinction between you and the Company, and that you wiſhed it only for the appearance it would have with the country powers ‡‡.

Your letter of the 27th is a matter of the utmoſt aſtoniſhment to me. In the public notice given, when the country of Tanjore was reſtored to the Raja, it was expreſsly ſaid, What he poſſeſſed at the concluſion of the treaty, *your Highneſs made* with him in 1762 §. No other was meant to be given to him, and the Raja never expreſſed a wiſh to have more than the Company thought his right.

* *This man* impoſed on his Lordſhip.

‡ A miſrepreſention throughout; as ſhall hereafter appear.

|| To carry a man *priſoner* is merely *eſcorting* him, in his Lordſhip's language.

§§ He means the *Carnatic*, by the *Payen-Ghaut*. A *vulgar* appellation is beneath the dignity of *heroics*; Payen-Ghaut may be underſtood in India, but it requires *explanation* to thoſe who are to *decide* here upon his Lordſhip's conduct.

‡‡ In this *inflated* and *arrogant* paragraph, his Lordſhip has permitted his *dignity* to get the better of *common prudence*.

§ His Lordſhip *made it*, and *forced* his Highneſs to ſign it.

Najib

Najib Khan received every mark of reſpect when he left Tanjore; and I aſſure your Highneſs, that every officer and ſervant I have ſeen of yours has merited and has received all the civility I could poſſibly pay to them.

I could ſay more in reply to this letter, but ſhall conclude with giving you the ſtrongeſt aſſurances of my ſteady *attachment to your intereſts*, and of the wiſh I have, that you would put it in my power to render you every ſervice I am capable of; being with the greateſt eſteem,

Your Highneſs's ſincere Friend,
and humble Servant,
(Signed) PIGOT.

Fort St. George,
13th May, 1776.

The Nabob anſwers the harſh letter which he received from Lord Pigot on the 13th of May. This paper is curious. Nine lacks of Pagodas, or 360,000*l.* are miſſing; and the letter is garbled by his Lordſhip.

Tranſlation of a Letter from his Highneſs the Nabob to Lord Pigot, dated 19th May 1776, or 30th Rabbelowell 1190.

I Have received your Lordſhip's letter in Engliſh, dated the 13th inſtant. I will hereafter particularly anſwer to the articles therein contained, and at preſent only obſerve, that you mention that "you have been informed "by the Dobbier, that the revenues of Tanjore, for this preſent year, have "amounted to only twelve lacks of pagodas, of which there remained only "three lacks to be collected by the Raja; and that my receipts, tunkas, and "the uſual charge, amounted to full nine, which gave you great ſatisfaction, "as you truſt that it will enable me to pay the arrears due to my troops;" which I underſtand.

I think it neceſſary, for your Lordſhip's better information, to acquaint you, that I had aſſigned part of the country for the payment of debts due to [Mr. Benfield and Mr. Monkton, to Mr. Benfield] *ſome perſons*; *to one*, a ſum amounting, by computation, to about five lacks and twenty-five thouſand pagodas; and to [Mr. Monkton] *another*, about three lacks of pagodas, beſides intereſt. *They* [theſe Gentlemen] have ſolemnly aſſured me, that they have received only, the firſt, about 12,750 pagodas; the other, about 8,500 pagodas. The Sepoys and other Tunkahdars may have received, in the ſame

ſame manner, however, the revenues (whatever they were) have not been paid, either to my creditors, to my Sepoys, or into my treaſury. Your Lordſhip [and your Counſellors] may eaſily inform [yourſelves] *yourſelf* how the money has been diſpoſed of.

This has been due to the Dobbier, who was *good enough* to ſay, that only a balance of *three lacks* of pagodas remained to be collected. If he ſhould ſay, that not a ſingle grain was left in the country, who can ſtop his mouth? If the revenues have been collected in the manner you mention in your letter, and that they amount to twelve lacks of pagodas, I am only informed of *three lacks* having been collected, and I have received credit for no more in my accounts.

Whatever the balance is, it *ſhould* be in the country————

May 22d, 1776. *N. B.* This letter was ſent to his Lordſhip on the day of the date; and after keeping it *three days*, he returned it to his Highneſs, and deſired that the alterations ſhould be made as above. It was therefore *altered* according to his Lordſhip's deſire, and this day ſent to him. The words between the brackets were in the firſt letter, in the room of which his lordſhip deſired to be put the words which are in Italics.

The Nabob finding that his dominions were invaded, and his ſubjects impriſoned, by the orders of Lord Pigot, wrote the following letter to an Engliſh officer in his ſervice.

Letter from the Nabob to Captain John Fletcher. May 21ſt, 1776.

To Captain John Fletcher.

THE fort of Haneemuntagoody is dependent upon Ramnade, and not upon Tanjore. If you have not delivered up that fort to the Company's people before the receipt of this letter, you are hereby directed not to deliver it up to them. You will take care not to fire any muſquetry or guns upon the Company's people, who may be ordered on that ſervice, nor to draw a ſword againſt them, but to keep the gates of the fort ſhut up, and to acquaint the Company's people, in a civil manner, that you have written to the Nabob, and deſire that they will wait until his anſwer arrives. In

the

the mean time I will apply to the Governor and Council here, and will inform you ſoon what you are to do.

What can I ſay more?

Given at Chepaugh,
21ſt May, 1776.

It appears from the following anſwer, that Captain Fletcher executed his Highneſs's orders.

Copy of a Letter from Captain Fletcher, from Hunmuntgoody, to the Nabob, dated 28th May, 1776.

To his Highneſs the Nabob Waulaujah Behauder, &c. &c.

I Received your Highneſs's letter, dated May the 21ſt, and will take the greateſt care that I will obey your Highneſs's orders, as far as lays in my power. I wrote two letters to Captain Rumley, to be explained to your Highneſs, mentioning the whole that happened here in this country. As I knew that Captain Rumley could explain it well to your Highneſs, on account of his knowing the Perſian language, which I hope he has long before now. I aſſure your Highneſs, that I will do every thing that lays in my power to ſerve you.

The Company's troops left this on the 20th inſtant, on account of their not getting admittance here. I have not heard of any of the Company's troops ſince.

Remaining, with reſpect,
Your Highneſs's moſt faithful Servant,
(Signed) JOHN FLETCHER, Captain.

Huntamongoody,
28th May, 1776.

The following very ſpirited letter was written by the Nabob to Lord Pigot, upon his Lordſhip's ſending the Company's troops to ſeize territories which *never belonged* to Tanjore; and to put them in the hands of the reſtored Raja.

Tranſlation

Translation of a Letter from his Highness the Nabob to Lord Pigot, dated 26th May 1776, or 17th Rabbisauny 1190 Hegira.

WHEN your Lordship was at Tanjore, I gave positive orders to my managers in that country, not to oppose the Company's people. I was soon after informed, that troops belonging to the Company were marched to take possession of some of my countries belonging to Ramanadeporam. As I had not sent any orders to my managers at Ramanadeporam, and God only knew what might happen there, I wrote to Mr. Stratton who then presided here, expressing my concern and asking his advice. I have lately repeatedly received letters from Aly Navas Cawn, and Attau Hussein Cawn, managers of the Ramanade and Shevagunga countries, mentioning the arrival of a Company's officer, with two companies of their Sepoys and some of Tuljagee's people, to take possession of some districts of those countries; and further, that they intend taking the Fort of Hanumuntagoody. Some of the Company's Sepoys are arrived at Cuttapatnam, and have *forcibly turned out my people* from thence; and have seized and carried away the Amildar, and possessed themselves of the *revenues* and the *papers*. Surely your Lordship should acquaint me before you proceed to take *possession of countries*, which do *not belong to Tanjore*, but entirely depend on Ramanade and Shevagunga, and you should examine the *records*, for the *word* of Tuljagee is not sufficient authority for taking possession of *my country*; but you *disregard all rights!* My firm friendship towards the Company for these thirty years past, has been founded on the strongest attachment to them and to the English nation; and from thence I have lived in the hope of increasing my honour, reputation and figure in the world; and which I trust you will consider as inseparably connected with the honour and interest of the Company.—I am perfectly convinced, that the Gentlemen of the Company will not allow me thus to *suffer*, nor see injustice done me; and I am firmly persuaded, that as soon as they have a *full* and *true state* of affairs here, they will alter their opinion in regard to Tanjore; then why should you desire to take my other countries?—I therefore write to your Lordship, that you will be pleased to give strict orders to your people, that my rights may be preserved, and that they may not interfere in my authority over my countries; for surely it never could have been the intention of the Company, that I, who have been their invariably firm friend,

for

for such a course of years, should meet with such treatment; and that one § who *never was a friend to the English*, but on the contrary their enemy, should meet with such advantage from their power.

In consequence of the preceding letter, Lord Pigot waited upon the Nabob at eight o'clock next morning, and had the following conference with his Highness, in the presence of his brother and two sons.

Translation of a Conference between his Highness the Nabob and Lord Pigot, May 27th 1776.

ON Monday morning about eight o'clock, his Lordship came to his Highness's house; Morphus Cawn * Behauder, Umdet-ul-Omrah, and Omeer-ul-Omrah Behauder †, received him; his Lordship, after inquiring about his Highness's health, said, that his Highness had yesterday wrote a letter to him, and asked why he had not previously seen it; that he did not *know* what were the bounds of Tanjore, and what were the bounds of Marawar; that he had given orders to put the Raja into possession of such countries as were in his hands at the treaty of 1762. His Lordship afterwards drew four lines on the ground, saying, here is the country of Trichinopoly, here the country of Tanjore, here the country of Marawar, and here the country of Tondyman; and said, that when the Raja of Tanjore became a little powerful, he took possession of some part of the Marawar country; and that when the Raja of Marawar became powerful, he took possession of part of the Tanjore country; that when the Tondyman became powerful, he took some part of the Tanjore country; that sometimes the Nabob took possession of the whole!—His Lordship then said, that the Nabob did not cultivate friendship with him; that there were several *great rascals*, such as Fletcher *, Mackay †, Benfield and Macpherson ‡, coming to his Highness, and that they spoiled him; that he (his Lordship) would stop such *rascals*, and that Benfield should not hereafter have it in his power

§ The Raja of Tanjore. * The Nabob's brother. † The Nabob's sons.

* Sir Robert Fletcher commander in chief of the Company's troops on the coast.

† A member of the Council.

‡ This Gentleman was *irregularly* dismissed from the service by Lord Pigot under a pretence that he PRESUMED, *before he was in the Company's service*, to endeavour the establishing a correspondence between the Crown of Great Britain and its ally, the Nabob of Arcot.

(even

(even upon his own business) to set his foot in his Highness's house. This his Lordship spoke loudly that every one heard it, and he *trembled* with passion. He was in this situation, when his Highness came to receive his visit; and stood in the same place, speaking very *harsh* and *severe words* to his Highness, such as that he would *place a guard of Europeans* on his Highness's house and *keep him in prison*, and in his *own power*, and would not allow any *white-faced rascal* to see his Highness §. He asked Umdat-ul-Omrah, why he did not *kick out* all such *rascals*. They afterwards sat down on chairs, and his Lordship repeatedly mentioned the same words; and that the whole settlement of Madras could not hurt him, had they a mind so to do; that he would not suffer the Company's business to be in confusion. His Highness said, that he (his Highness) was a friend to the Company, and would not be the cause of spoiling their business. His Lordship said, that such letters as his Highness formerly wrote him were replete with wisdom, but that now they were full of trouble and disturbance; for the draughts of them were *made out by rascals* *: and further, that the Nabob should have told him yesterday, that the Company's people were about taking possession of his countries, and that his Lordship should stop them; and that if his Highness had done so, he (his Lordship) would have given him a friendly answer, and would have told his Highness, that he would have sent orders to stop this business †; that if the Nabob wanted to see him and ask his advice, he should not let any other people come to him; but if he (his Highness) did not think proper to see him, he would not come to him, but would appoint one of the Council to come and talk to his Highness. That one ship was gone to England full of his Highness's praise; and declaring, that he had *agreed* to every thing ‡; but that every ship since had gone to England full of complaints from his Lordship against his Highness.

§ His Lordship afterwards found it convenient to *find* another reason for this threat. In his minute of the 6th of June, he tells a story concerning a *poor woman*, who was to be tortured for her *wealth*; a piece of intelligence which he received on the 10th of May from one of the Company's *black porters*. Whether this woman ever existed is best known to his Lordship and his *black porter*; but if his humanity was so much alarmed on the 10th of May, it is somewhat surprising he did not bring forward the fact till the end of the first week of June.

* His Highness sends no letter of business which he does not himself dictate to his Moonshy.

† He acknowledges here the injustice of his own conduct.

‡ His Lordship had no authority for such a declaration, his Highness uniformly dissented from the measure of restoring Tanjore.

nefs. That his Lordfhip had no more friendfhip with the Raja than with his Highnefs, but had replaced him purfuant to the orders of the Company. That his Highnefs fhould do one favour now, to fend a perfon from him with orders, that the Raja fhould have delivered into his poffeffion, fuch countries as he had in 1762, and that then there would be no difference between his Highnefs and his Lordfhip. That his Highnefs mentioned fomething in his letter about Hanumuntagoody, which had been, fince former times, in the poffeffion of the Raja. His Highnefs replied, that Hanumuntagoody belonged to the country of Ramnade. His Lordfhip then faid, why did your Highnefs not mention this bufinefs when the treaty of 1762 was fettled? His Highnefs anfwered, that he imagined that it regarded only the Tanjore country, and that he did not imagine that it extended to all.—His Lordfhip then ftood up and told his Highnefs, that he (his Highnefs) fhould *forgive his fault* in fpeaking fome high and *violent words*; for that they proceeded from his *hearty friendfhip*. His Highnefs anfwered, that he was a friend to the Company, and would only anfwer to all his Lordfhip had faid, that after fo long enjoying the friendfhip of the Company and the Englifh nation, he had no expectation of *deferving fuch words!* His Lordfhip then faid, that his Highnefs fhould forgive him, for he had *fpoken through madnefs*; but his Highnefs made no reply *.

Lord Pigot having threatened, in the preceding conference with the Nabob, to place a guard of Europeans on his Highnefs's houfe, and to *keep him in prifon* and in his *own power*; that unfortunate prince, as his laft refuge from difgrace, found himfelf obliged to make the following application to Sir Edward Hughes, commander in chief of his Majefty's fquadron in the Eaft Indies.

Letter from his Highnefs the Nabob to Commodore Sir Edward Hughes, June 3d, 1776.

THE affurances of fupport and protection received from the grandfather of his prefent Majefty, and repeatedly from his Majefty himfelf, and the Company, had given me the greateft confidence, that my *rights* and

* The latter part of this conference is particularly recommended to the attention of the reader.

my

my *honour* would have been preſerved inviolate; but the apprehenſions under which I now labour, from Lord Pigot's unjuſt uſe of his power, have arrived at ſo dangerous a height, that I am obliged to apply to you, for your immediate interference in my ſupport.

Lord Pigot, not content with the *low* and *diſgraceful ſtate*, to which he has reduced my authority, by the meaſures which he executed at Tanjore, has lately threatened to ſubject me to the moſt perſonal diſgrace.

On the 27th inſtant, at eight o'clock in the morning, he came to my Durbar, and in the preſence of my brother Morpheus Cawn Behawder, and my ſons Omdaht-ul-Omrah Behawder, and Ameer-ul-Omrah Behawder, and Kirin Mordien Cawn, declared, in the moſt determined and *threatening tone of voice*, that he would place a European guard upon my houſe, *to keep me a priſoner* in his *own power*; and naming *members of the Council*, he ſaid they were *raſcals*, and that he would diſmiſs them from the ſervice; he ſaid alſo, that all the *white-faced fellows* were *raſcals*, and that he would not allow any of them to ſee me; alſo he aſked Ameer-ul-Omrah, why he did not kick out ſuch *raſcals*.

The cauſe of this outrage, was my having written him a letter on the 26th inſtant, a copy of which is encloſed, repreſenting the injuſtice which he did me, by ordering a military force to march into the Ramnade country, to deprive me of ſome diſtricts there, and put them into the poſſeſſion of Tuljagee.

Can there be any oppreſſion equal to the depriving a man of his right, and then threatening him with the greateſt diſgrace, if he dares to make a repreſentation of that right?

As Lord Pigot, on a former occaſion, ordered people to enter my garden in the middle of the night*, *pretending*, that he had information, that I had ordered ſome people to be ill-treated there; ſo I am under the greateſt alarm, that he will proceed to execute in *paſſion*, what he threatened. I ſhall then be without remedy. I value my *honour* more than my *life*; as

* This was in conſequence of the idle ſtory of the 10th of May, communicated by a malicious *porter* to Lord Pigot, concerning a *poor woman* who was to have been ſent to ſome diſtant country to be tortured for *her money*.

you are the servant of the King and nation, who are my protectors, as you are sent here for the support of *your Sovereign's honour* and the interest of the Company; so *I call upon you*, by every duty which you owe to justice, and your high station, to write immediately to the Board, and to settle such measures with them, that my *person* and *family* may be secured against Lord Pigot's *threats* and *violence*.

Such is the justice of my cause, that I am confident the Company will order me full redress for the injuries which have been done to my government and people by Lord Pigot's conduct at Tanjore; but who is to support me against those he threatens at present, unless you represent to the Council my situation. By the established custom, I cannot apply to the Council, but through the governor, and *my complaint is of himself*.

Unless you give immediate aid to the best friend the English ever found in India, he must sink in the sea of oppression.

I *solemnly declare*, and your knowledge of my conduct has proved it to you, that I am a *faithful friend* and *well-wisher* to HIS MAJESTY and the *Company*.

Sir Edward Hughes returned immediately the following answer.

Copy of a Letter from Sir Edward Hughes to his Highness, dated 3d June 1776.

To his Highness the Nabob.

May it please your Highness,

I Have this minute received your Highness's *public application* to me as his MAJESTY's *servant*, and forward the same directly to the Governor and Council. The distress under which your Highness labours affects me more than is in the power of words to express. I will use every effort in my power to support your Highness, being fully sensible, that in so doing, I shall act to the satisfaction of my SOVEREIGN and for the good of the Company.

I am certain, that your attachment to BOTH, and to the English nation, hath been hitherto invariable, and that it remains unquestionable.

I cannot

I cannot entertain a doubt, but that your Highneſs will obtain an immediate relief from your apprehenſions of any perſonal inſult, which I will hope was never really intended.

I have the honour to be,
with very great reſpect,
your Highneſs's moſt obedient,
and very humble ſervant,

St. Thome,
3d June 1776.

(Signed) Edward Hughes.

Sir Edward Hughes, at the ſame time, wrote the following letter, incloſing that of the Nabob, to the preſidency of Madras.

Copy of a letter from Sir Edward Hughes to Lord Pigot and Council, dated St. Thome, 3d June 1776.

To the Right Honourable George Lord Pigot Preſident, and Governor and Council, &c. &c. &c.

My Lord and Gentlemen,

IT is with the greateſt concern, that I find myſelf under the neceſſity of interfering in any reſpect, between the repreſentatives of the Company, and the Nabob of the Carnatic; but the accompanying application from his Highneſs, is of ſo *alarming a tendency*, that I cannot avoid laying it before you, as early as poſſible, part of the king's inſtructions to me, being to do my utmoſt to promote the intereſts of his Majeſty, and the advantage of the united Company of merchants trading to the Eaſt Indies, and of ſuch *Indian princes*, with whom they have contracted, or may contract engagements; of theſe the Nabob of the Carnatic holds the moſt diſtinguiſhed place.

My duty to the King my maſter, my zeal for the Company's welfare, and the feelings I have for the diſtreſſes of ſo good a friend to both, are with me moſt urgent motives for this addreſs; and I have no doubt, but that you will take ſuch meaſures in conſequence, as will effectually protect the Nabob from ſuch alarms in future. The national honour and intereſt, as well as the welfare of the Company, being materially connected with the juſt ſecurity of his Highneſs.

I have the honour to be,
my Lord and Gentlemen,
your moſt obedient and devoted
humble ſervant,
(Signed) Edward Hughes.

A true copy, Edward Spine, Sec.
To the Commander in chief.

The Preſident and Council returned, on the ſame day, the following anſwer.

Copy of a Letter from Lord Pigot and Council to Sir Edward Hughes, dated 3d June 1776.

To Sir Edward Hughes, Commander in Chief of his Majeſty's Ships in India.

SIR,

WE have the honour of your letter of this day. Our Preſident aſſures us, "that the Nabob has totally *miſunderſtood him* *; that he never "had a thought of placing any guard over him, although he feared, and "expreſſed thoſe fears to the Nabob, that the encouragement his Highneſs "gave to *European viſitors*, and the impediments to public buſineſs, ariſing "from the *intrigues* carried on by them at his Durbar, would lay him under "a neceſſity to place a guard to *bring ſuch perſons to him*; that he might be "acquainted with the nature of their buſineſs."

We conclude this will be ſufficient to ſatisfy you, Sir, that the Nabob's perſon is in perfect ſecurity. Our Preſident declares, "that no wanton in-"dignity to his Highneſs ever was intended †, or ever will be committed, by "him, although his ears can never be ſhut to the complaints of the *diſ-*"*treſſed* ‡," and we aſſure you that no ſuch indignity to the Nabob ſhall

* This is very unlikely. The conference on his Lordſhip's part was held in Engliſh; the Nabob underſtands that language very well; and beſides, the words were *taken down* to be interpreted, in the uſual form, in Perſian.

† Whence then proceeded his threats in the conference of the 27th May?

‡ Vide Lord Pigot's minute of the 6th June, which immediately follows the ſucceeding letter in this collection.

be countenanced by this Board, to whom the management of the Company's affairs on this coaſt is intruſted.

We have the honour to be, with the greateſt eſteem,

Fort St, George,
3d June 1776.

SIR,

Your moſt obedient humble Servants,

(Signed) PIGOT, GEO. STRATTON, ROB. FLETCHER, GE. DAWSON, HENRY BROOKE, CLAUD RUSSEL, A. DALRYMPLE, J. M. STONE, ARCHDALE PALMER, FRANCIS JOURDAN, GEO. MACKAY.

When Lord (then Mr.) Pigot was formerly Governor of Madras, he *gave a river*, belonging to the Nabob of Arcot, to his *own friend* Pertaub Sing, Raja of Tanjore. He now ſends the following letter to Lieutenant Colonel Harper, military Commandant at Tanjore, to prevent the river from being brought back to its *old channel*. There was, however, no foundation for his Lordſhip's fears.

Copy of a Letter from Lord Pigot and Council, to Colonel Harper, dated 3d June 1776,

To Lieutenant Colonel Harper, commanding at Tanjore.

SIR,

YOU will forthwith direct Major Stevens to proceed to the iſland of Seringham, to inſpect the water channels carrying on by the Nabob; and if it ſhould appear to him that there is any immediate danger therefrom to the Tanjore country, he will repreſent the ſame to Colonel James.

We are,

Fort St. George,
3d June 1776.

SIR,

Your moſt obedient Servants,

PIGOT, and Council.

(A true Copy.) R. J. SULIVAN, Secretary.

Lord Pigot, in the letter to Sir Edward Hughes, had mentioned, that " his ears " can never be ſhut to the complaints of the *diſtreſſed*." The ſentiment is laudable, where diſtreſs really exiſts. Upon the information of one of the Company's black porters, concerning a *poor woman* who was ſaid to be threatened with the torture for her *money*, his Lordſhip committed an outrage, of which the Nabob complains, in his letter to Sir Edward Hughes, of the 3d of June. The Nabob ſays, " Lord Pigot, on a former occaſion, ordered people to " enter my garden, in the middle of the night, PRETENDING that he had " information that I had ordered ſome people to be ill-treated there." What became of the woman, or *whether ſhe ever exiſted*, he is wiſe, indeed, who can tell. The Hircarrah ſeems to have impoſed upon his Lordſhip *entirely*, or, at leaſt, to have very much miſrepreſented the facts.

C O P Y.

The Preſident's Explanation, in Conſultation 6th June, of a Complaint made in the Nabob's Letter to Sir Ed. Hughes.

Minute of the Preſident, delivered in 6th June 1776.

THE Preſident then obſerves, that there was, in the letter from the Nabob to Sir Ed. Hughes, an accuſation of his having ordered people, in the middle of the night, to enter the Nabob's garden, pretending that he had information of the Nabob's having ordered ſome people to be ill-treated there.

The Preſident adds, that he thought moſt of the Members of the Council had been acquainted with the caſe alluded to; and although he had wiſhed, for the credit of the Nabob, to have taken no public notice thereof, yet for his (the Preſident's) vindication, it appears neceſſary to mention at this time.

On the 10th of May he received the following report from the Head Hircarrah.

Report of the Head Hircarrah.

After the Nabob took the Marawar's Country, the Circar's people plundered every thing belonging to the ſaid Marawar's managers; among the reſt,

reſt, one Vellayan Chirrocar's houſe was plundered, and his daughter remained in the ſaid country very poor.

One Vurrapilla, an enemy to her, told the Nabob that ſhe was worth money; upon which he ordered her to be brought under guard to him, and accordingly ſhe and two more women, and about 13 men, were brought to Chepauk, the Company's bounds, a few days ago; but upon examining the women, there was no money to be got from her, as expected; on this, the ſaid enemy told the Nabob, that if he would ſend her back along with him to the ſaid country, he will put her to the torture and recover the money. The woman could not go for fear they would murder her; but they are forcing her to go, and ſhe declares, that if ſhe is forced ſhe will kill herſelf. As ſhe is now in the Company's bounds, ſent to acquaint your Lordſhip with the above violence, and beg you to ſave her life; and as it is my duty to acquaint you with any news or violence that might be committed in the bounds, I thought fit to make this report to your Lordſhip.

The Preſident was upon a viſit, and at ſupper, when he received this information, and as the Nabob's gardens and thoſe to the Company's houſe join, he ordered the Hircarrah to wait at the gardens till his return, and to watch if theſe people paſſed; about eleven o'clock, the Preſident ſtopping at the gardens, in his way to the fort, was informed that the woman was not come away, but that ſome of the people were carried off towards St. Thome; upon which the Preſident thought proper to direct the officer of the guard to ſend a Havildar and ſome Sepoys, who overtook them at St. Thome; and the Preſident, at the ſame time, gave to Sail, one of the Company's waiting Peons, the written information he had received, and directed him to carry it to a houſe of the Nabob's, where many of his ſervants generally are, and to deſire that the woman might not be removed till he ſaw the Nabob in the morning †.

(A true Copy.) D. Baine, Dep. Mil. Sec.

Though Lord Pigot neglected to communicate his proceedings at Tanjore, to the Supreme Council at Bengal, they had received information of the hoſtilities and outrages, which his Lordſhip had choſen

† There does not appear to have been the ſlighteſt foundation for this idle tale.

to

to commit within the territories of the Nabob. The following letter was therefore ſent from Bengal, on the 15th of May; and it was received at Madras early in the month of June. The Supreme Council conſider his Lordſhip's conduct, in invading the Nabob's territories, and ſeizing the perſons of his officers, " a violation of the independent RIGHTS of the " Nabob of the Carnatic; in which character Mahomet Ally Cawn is ac- " knowledged by the TREATY OF PARIS; and that the tranſaction is not " warranted by the *Company's orders*."

Letter from the Supreme Council, May 15th 1776.

To the Right Honourable George Lord Pigot, Preſident, &c. Council at Fort St. George.

My Lord and Gentlemen,

WE have been favoured with your letter of the 15th April.

The Court of Directors having been pleaſed to tranſmit to us a copy of their letter to your Preſidency, dated 12th April 1775, containing their commands on ſundry very important regulations and arrangements for the conduct of their political intereſts in the Carnatic, and expreſsly commanding us to co-operate with you, and to yield you our aſſiſtance in bringing them to a ſpeedy and happy concluſion;

We have waited with great impatience to this time for your advices, with reſpect to *the manner in which you have carried thoſe orders into execution*; but have hitherto received *no information* in any way relating to them, except the ſummary intelligence contained in your letters of the 17th February and 29th March, that the ſubſtance of the Company's orders, relative to Tanjore, had been communicated to that Raja; that a garriſon of the Company's forces had been admitted to relieve the Nabob's troops in that fort; and that your Preſident had ſet out for Tanjore, for the purpoſe of carrying the Company's orders into effect; but to this time we are totally uninformed of all the previous and intermediate meaſures and reſolutions, which have been taken for the accompliſhment of the various objects of this general ſubject, recommended in the general letter abovementioned; and of the *negotiations* which have paſſed between the *Preſident*

and

and the *Nabob* and *Raja*. We therefore DESIRE, that you will tranſmit to us copies of *all your proceedings*, which have a relation to this object of your inſtructions, as well as copies of all your correſpondence on the ſame ſubject, with your Preſident, ſince his departure.

We are the more deſirous of receiving theſe *materials*, as we are informed, that an officer at the head of the Company's troops, had been ſent to Eleanore †, which we underſtand is ſituated *without the boundary of the kingdom of Tanjore*, to ſeize upon one or more of the Nabob's officers, and had carried him or them with their papers to Tanjore. This act requires *explanation*. If it was *neceſſary*, in order to carry the Company's intentions into execution, you will be juſtified by your inſtructions. But this tranſaction, as far as we are yet acquainted with it, appears to us, *a violation of the independent rights of the Nabob of the Carnatic*; in which character Mahomet Ally Cawn is acknowledged by the TREATY OF PARIS; and that it is not *warranted* by the Company's orders.

We farther deſire, that you will cauſe copies to be made of all the treaties which are now in force between your Preſidency and any of the country powers, or which may at any time have been guaranteed by you, and tranſmit them to us by the firſt opportunity.

We are,
My Lord and Gentlemen,
Your moſt obedient humble ſervants,

Fort William,
the 15th May 1776.

WARREN HASTINGS,
J. CLAVERING,
GEORGE MONSON,
RICHARD BARWELL.

(A true Copy) D. BAINE, Dep. Mil. Sec.

In anſwer to the preceding *requiſitorial letter*, from Bengal, the preſidency wrote the following, on the 13th of June. Lord Pigot endeavours to explain away his own acts of hoſtility at Arialore. He leaves the Supreme Council to *find out* his other outrages of the ſame kind.

† Arialore.

The Answer of the Presidency of Madras to the Letter of the Supreme Council.

To the Honourable Warren Hastings, Esq; Governor General, &c. Council of Fort William in Bengal.

Honourable Sir and Sirs,

WE have had the honour to receive your letter of the 15th May.

Incapable as we are of being intentionally wanting in *respect* to you, or deficient in our *duty*, we thought the information contained in our letters of the 17th February and 29th March, respecting Tanjore, was all which was material at that time; our political situation has undergone no change, except with respect to Tanjore; and our letter of the 14th May, contains a full account of the Raja's request, and our resolution thereupon. But as you are pleased to desire to have a copy of all our proceedings *, in relation to Tanjore, the same shall be transmitted with all convenient expedition.

Our President acquaints us, " That as he passed through the Tanjore " country, he found the proper officers, with all the accounts, had been re- " moved by the Nabob's orders from the villages †, and was soon informed, " that every part of the country was in the same situation; that every means " had been taken to throw difficulties in his way in the execution of the " Company's orders, and to distress the country and inhabitants. That " without the assistance of the Dobeer and his accounts, it would have " been impossible for the Raja to have obtained any knowledge of the re- " venues, or indeed to have been properly placed in the management of " his country; this man having been first minister, and in fact *governed* " *the Tanjore country* ‡ for these fifty years past. After Tanjore was taken, " he told the Nabob's second son, who commanded there for his father, " that he would not desert his master in his misfortunes, and refused to act,

* The proceedings of the Council were not *material*. They were ordered implicitly to obey the injunctions given by the Directors, relative to Tanjore. The *material* correspondence passed between the Nabob and Lord Pigot; but as his Lordship has not chosen to transmit that correspondence to the Court of Directors, it is not to be supposed he will be more complaisant to the Supreme Council.

† Yet the Nabob had assured his Lordship, that the accounts of every village were to be found in itself. His Lordship was not at the trouble of enquiring.

‡ What then became of the authority of his Lordship's *old friend Pertaub Sing?* What of the prerogatives of his *Majesty* Tuljagee?

" until

" until he carried him to the Raja, and desired the Raja to lay his com-
" mands upon him. On his (the president's) proceeding for Tanjore, the
" Nabob ordered the Dobeer to be sent out of the Tanjore country, with
" all the public accounts. The Dobeer had retarded his journey by va-
" rious pretences, and sent a message to the Raja, desiring that he might
" be conducted to Tanjore. The troop which attended the president, was
" therefore sent to escort him; but when the troop arrived at the place,
" whence the message to the Raja had been sent, they found the Dobeer
" had been conveyed from thence to Arialore; whither the commanding
" officer of the troop followed, and escorted him to Tanjore.

" Our president wrote the Nabob, that if he would please to order the
" several Amildars and other officers, to return with their accounts to the
" Dobeer of Tanjore, justice might be done to every man, and the coun-
" try restored in a proper and equitable manner. The Nabob, however,
" to this day, has not been pleased to do so."

Our president adds, " he has always endeavoured to transact the business
" of the Company, in the manner most *agreeable to the Nabob* *, but his
" rule has ever been, that the *Company's business must be done.*"

We *will* never lose sight of the *treaty of Paris*; but we cannot believe, that treaty can be construed to obstruct any proper measure, which may be necessary for the Company's *security*, or the *safety* of the Carnatic †.

We have the honour to enclose you an extract of our honourable Masters orders to this presidency *per* Royal Henry, dated the 25th November 1775, and also of the general letter from England received by the Lord Camden. We have no advices from you on the subject, to which this letter relates, since your letter of the 7th March, &c.

We have the houour to be,
Honourable Sir and Sirs,
your most obedient, and most humble servants,

Fort St. George,
13th June, 1776.

PIGOT, &c. Council.

[A true copy] D. BAINE, Dep. Mil. Sec.

* Witness the whole of the preceding conferences and letters!!!

† This is a *new* axiom in politics, that *hostility* and *invasion* are necessary for the *security* and *safety* of a country.

O Though

Though Lord Pigot, in his conference with the Nabob, on the 27th of May, when his Lordſhip flew into indecent fits of paſſion, deſired his Highneſs "*to forgive his fault*, for he had *ſpoken through madneſs*;" he ſeems to have relapſed into his former *rage*, upon the Nabob's application to Sir Edward Hughes, for protection. The ſtory concerning the *poor woman*, being litle credited, his Lordſhip had recourſe to a tale he had heard about *children*. This tale, upon being canvaſſed, fell alſo to the ground. The Nabob had never heard of the children, nor was the man in his ſervice. The perſon who had the children, was a merchant, a native of Arcot, and had long dealt in that ſpecies of commerce; which is commom in the eaſt, though not practiſed in Europe. It appeared, that this child-merchant had bought the children from their parents, and had treated them with great care and humanity; the Nabob, however, upon being informed of the circumſtances, ordered the children to be releaſed, gave them money, and ſent them back to their parents.

Extract of Minutes of Conſultation, 17th June 1776.

THE Preſident repreſents to the Board the many difficulties that attend the conſtant reſidence of the Nabob within the Company's bounds, from the frequent acts committed, which are incompatible with our laws.

Inſtances of murder, impriſonments, thefts, tortures, and ſuch like offences committed by the Nabob's people, wherein the interference of this Government is indiſpenſably neceſſary, have already happened in the ſhort time the Preſident has been here. He ſhould ill deſerve the truſt repoſed in him, if he let information of ſuch a nature paſs unnoticed; and if he is not paſſive, the Nabob will ever think his dignity hurt *.

Another inconvenience ariſes from the ſuits in the Mayor's court, againſt the Nabob's family and attendants, which occaſion applications that muſt lay the Preſident under the greateſt embarraſſment.

* Theſe general accuſations will gain little credit till facts are proved.

The Nabob has not mentioned it in his letter to Sir Edward Hughes, but the Prefident knows well he was moft chagrin'd at the Prefident's having releafed fome children, ftolen by a Moorman, *formerly*, if not at prefent in the Nabob's fervice, and who was ftopt in the Company's bounds, but conveyed away by the Nabob's officers into his Highnefs's country, and thereby has eluded the juftice of the Englifh laws. Of thefe children nineteen were taken from the Tanjore country, one from St. Thome, and two from Cuddalore.

The Prefident being defirous to avoid every occafion of *giving difguft to the Nabob*, and as circumftances muft occur daily to increafe his difcontent whilft he remains here, the Prefident propofes as the moft effectual method to prevent thefe mifunderftandings, that it be recommended to the Nabob to refide at Arcot †.

Agreed that the Prefident be defired to addrefs a letter to the Nabob to that effect.

Carried againft the queftion 7 to 5.

(A true extract) D. BAINE, Dep. Mil. Sec.

The following is Mr. Mackay's opinion on the Prefident's minute, inferted in the draught of the general letter par. 8. PROPOSED by the Prefident, but *rejected* by a majority of the Council. The Prefident's words were, "the "Prefident recommends, that agreeable to the Company's ftanding orders, "no member of the Council do henceforth *vifit*, or correfpond by *writing* or "by *meffage*, with the Nabob, or either of his fons."

Extract of Minutes of Confultation, 17th June 1776.

I Put my negative on the Prefident's queftion, becaufe I think the Court of Directors do not mean, that the Nabob fhould be prevented from feeing any perfon whatever, much lefs members of this Government. I con-

† This ftrange motion was furely the effect of paffion; and it met with the fate it deferved. It had been uniformly the policy of former Governors and Councils to encourage the Nabob to live at Madras, that they might partake in his councils; his interefts and thofe of the Britifh nation were infeparable.

 ceive

ceive these orders must only mean that all correspondence with the Nabob, and other country powers on their affairs, should be carried on by the President, and nothing more.

I apprehend, that making an order now, that members of the Council should not visit the Nabob, would be extremely improper, and more especially as *accusations* from the Nabob *against the President* are now before the Board.

GEORGE MACKAY.

As a sequel to the preceding papers, relative to Tanjore, it is thought proper to print the general letter in the military department, on the same subject. The letter from the Raja, alluded to, is subjoined; it being judged improper, to break the chain of the correspondence between the Nabob and Lord Pigot, by placing it in the order of time. In this letter of the Council, in their military department, they seem to *approve* of Lord Pigot's conduct at Tanjore. They afterwards disapproved of the *whole of the President's conduct*, when at that place. This contradiction, in the sentiments of the members, proceeded from their being better informed *afterwards*, than on the 14th of May.

General Letter from Fort St. George.

To the Honourable the Court of Directors, &c.

Military Department, May 14th 1776.

WE paid our respects to you by the Ankerwyke and Hilsborough, under date the 14th February, and then acquainted you, that the Nabob had admitted your troops into the garrison of Tanjore the 9th of that month.

No persuasions however could induce him to concur in restoring the Raja. He said he would not *oppose the execution of your orders*, but would never consent to give up the Tanjore country. So circumstanced, we determined, in consequence of the order you had been pleased to send us by the Grenville, to restore the Raja by your authority; and we thought proper to entrust the execution of those orders to our President. He set out the 30th of of March, and returned from Tanjore the 5th of May; and we have now the pleaſure to tell you, that the Raja is put into poſſeſſion of the whole country his father held in 1762, when the treaty was concluded with the Nabob *.

His fort is not only garriſoned by your troops, but his country protected by them alſo; He has on this account engaged to pay into your caſh 400,000 pagodas annually, and will keep no other troops himſelf, but what are neceſſary for his guards, the number not to exceed 500. We have the greater ſatisfaction in informing you of this, as every meaſure we have taken has been at *his requeſt*.

And the encloſed copy of the Raja's letter, will, we flatter ourſelves, give you perfect ſatisfaction. We did not think it right to accept any additional country near † Devicotah. We have complied with the Raja's requeſt in all other reſpects, and our Preſident begs leave to aſſure you, that he cannot expreſs how grateful the Raja is for the juſtice you have done, nor how much he merits your countenance and protection.

Fort St. George,
14th May, 1776.

We are, *&c.*

PIGOT.	A. DALRYMPLE.
GEO. STRATTON.	W. STONE.
ROBT. FLETCHER.	ARCHDALE PALMER.
G. DAWSON.	FRANCIS JOURDAN.
HENRY BROOK.	GEO. MACKAY.
CLAUD RUSSEL.	

The day after the ceremony of the reſtoration at Tanjore, Lord Pigot ſays he *received* the following letter from the Raja. As his Lordſhip offered frequently *his ſervices* to the Nabob of Arcot, to write letters to himſelf (as has appeared in the preceding part of this collection), we can form no doubt but either he or his ſecretary (or, *perhaps*, Mr. Dalrymple) *held the pen* for Tuljagee. This letter therefore may be con-

* So much ſtreſs has been laid upon this Treaty by Lord Pigot, that it was thought proper to print it in this collection.

† Becauſe, having taken the *whole country*, this became as ſuperfluous as the Preſident's expreſſions of the *Raja's gratitude*.

ſidered,

ſidered, as containing his *Lordſhip's ſentiments*, (rather than thoſe of his *man of ſtraw*,) or at leaſt what he wiſhed to hold forth to the Company as ſuch.

Copy of a Letter from the Raja of Tanjore, 12th April 1776.

THE ſatisfaction I feel on occaſion of ſuch a friendſhip and extraordinary juſtice as the Company have diſplayed towards me is ſo great, that were I to begin to tell you what my mind conceives on the occaſion, the ſubject would never have an end; had I a thouſand tongues, they could not expreſs my gratitude. When I had an interview with your Lordſhip, I opened to you the ſentiments of my heart; but as mere verbal declarations on this head are inſufficient, I have thought it proper to write you a letter.

I ſhall ever conſider myſelf as nouriſhed and protected by the Company, and ſhall therefore never *aſſiſt* or *ſuccour* their enemies *, no meaſure ſhall ever proceed from me, that is contrary to their intereſts; nor will I ever ſet on foot any connection with other powers, without the Company's conſent. This I have written as a means of increaſing the friendſhip that is between us. In the *preſent condition* of my country, the placing a garriſon of the Engliſh troops in the fort and city of Tanjore is *exceedingly neceſſary*; but beſides this garriſon, if the Company will allow ſome more troops likewiſe for the protection of my whole country, this alſo will be highly proper. If by the favour of Heaven this be put in execution, neither I or any of my family will need to apprehend that the calamities of war will fall upon this country again; and if the Company will only favour me thus far, I will with pleaſure aſſign them out of my revenues, the ſum of four lacks of pagodas *per annum*, for their military expences. The mode of payment as follows; November 20,000, December 40,000, January 40,000, February 100,000, March 100,000, April 100,000.

For my body-guard, I ſhall keep a body of men from one hundred to five hundred; and I want not to have one man either of horſe or foot, more than that number.

* This he had *ſworn* to do before; but he broke his *oath*.

As my finances are in utter diſorder, and the ſtate † of my country all in confuſion, I muſt throw myſelf on the Company for my preſent ſupport. I therefore wiſh them to *buy* of me at a reaſonable rate, all the grain of the preſent year, except what my country may be in need of. By this meaſure the Company will not be burthened, and I ſhall be enabled to defray the expences of my government, without running in debt.

Finally, as the Fort of Devecotah has no country annexed to it, I beg the Company will take what they think proper as a dependancy thereon.

The country of Tanjore is the Company's; I here only beg, that they will preſerve my honour.

Remarks on the Raja's Letter.

IT appeared, that Father Swartz, Colonel Harper and the Colonel's Debaſh, were the *penmen* of the epiſtolary correſpondence of the *King* of *Tanjore*, on the *leſſer affairs* of *his* KINGDOM; but this letter bears the mark of higher authority, being indubitably the performance of the *King*'s KING. The letter is ſo full of abſurdity, that it defeats the intention of the writer; and proves to demonſtration the *reverſe* of what he meant to inſinuate; viz. that the Raja is a *free agent*; and that he is *thankful* for the mode in which he has been reſtored. It proves alſo, what the Right Honourable writer did not mean to *prove*; that he has had *interviews* with the Raja, and that a *ſyſtem of corruption* is eſtabliſhed, by which *two thirds* of the revenues of the country may be ſunk into *private pockets*, WITHOUT ACCOUNT; and that individuals may occaſion a famine in the KINGDOM of Tanjore, under the pretence of buying, *for the Company*, the ſuperabundant grain at their *own price*.

What are the neceſſities, by the ſyſtem eſtabliſhed, which oblige the Raja to ſell the intire corn of his fertile country *at any* price? What are the bleſſings for which he is ſo thankful, that a thouſand tongues could not recount them?

† All the ſervants of the Nabob, placed for the management of the country and the collection of the revenues, had been removed by violence, and perſons choſen by Vincatachelum, Lord Pigot's Banyan or Debaſh, put in their ſtead.

The

The revenues of Tanjore amount to about 20 lacks of pagodas, or 800,000*l.* at leaſt annually; the Raja is not to maintain a ſingle ſoldier, the Company *at his requeſt* having undertaken to protect the whole, including the capital; and for this ſervice four lacks of pagodas, or 160,000*l.* are thought ſufficient: the ſurplus therefore is ſixteen lacks, for the 20 lacks *per annum* are clear of the charges of collection. Why then ſell all the grain of the country, at the hazard of a famine? Is the Raja to ſpend ſixteen lacks of pagodas, or 640,000*l.* *per annum*, in riot and debauchery? If not, what becomes of the corn and of theſe ſixteen lacks or 640,000*l.* annually? Lord Pigot, perhaps, can account for them. They are as eaſily accounted for, as any other part of his Lordſhip's conduct.

Under the Nabob's management, the Raja had every article of convenience, pleaſure, and luxury furniſhed him; and enjoyed a ſecurity, to which he had ever been a ſtranger, on account of the cruelty and oppreſſion of his adminiſtration.—What has Lord Pigot done more for him? He has given him a guard of 100 to 500 men, who will ſcarcely protect him better than thoſe who attended him before; and who will probably hold him equally a priſoner, without being *reſponſible* for his ſafety.

Whether the offer of receiving troops to *protect* the whole country of Tanjore originated from the Raja or his Right Honourable Reſtorer, is perfectly indifferent; but the meaſure will bring the Company to ſhame let who will be the author of it, being in itſelf a direct breach of the *national Guarantee*, the Company having thereby ſeized for their *own uſe* the moſt conſiderable diſtrict of the Carnatic, *in violation of the Nabob's independent rights*, which they were bound by treaty to preſerve.—The Raja, if capable of reaſoning, reaſoned thus; "You have ſeized my fortreſs of Tanjore, you may as well "ſeize more; I am a priſoner in my capital and cannot govern my country, "take therefore what land you think proper, as a dependency on Devicotah;" nay, take the whole. "*The country of Tanjore is the Company's, I* "*have only to beg, that they will preſerve my honour* †."

However the Governor and Council at Madras may plume themſelves on ſuch conduct as this; however the Directors at home may approve of ſuch ſervants; the King, the Parliament, and the nation, in whoſe name the Nabob implored the *clemency* of Lord Pigot in vain; and to whom he has now

† See the preceding letter, from the Raja.

made his solemn appeal will, it is to be hoped, for the honour of the nation, attend to the faith of treaties and the call of justice; and bring the abusers of delegated powers, the usurpers of sovereignty, to condign and speedy punishment.

The best comment upon the following letter is the extract of the letter from the Presidency, of the same date, which is subjoined to it. The first letter is manifestly intended to give an *impression*; but an antidote is annexed to the poison, by the majority of the Council.

Extract of a Letter proposed *by the President to be written by Administration here; followed by a Letter from the President to Court of Directors.*

Fort St. George, 22d *June* 1776.

SHOULD you have received a short letter we wrote you the 14th of May, you will be surprised to find, that *the whole of your President's conduct, during the time he was at Tanjore*, has since been disapproved by a majority of the Council. By the Grenville we shall transmit to you our Proceedings *complete*; in the mean while we think it necessary to say something on the subject of our divisions.

We inclose a letter from Mr. Paul Benfield, dated 19th May, upon which it was that day resolved, that the Raja of Tanjore being put in the full possession of his country by the Company's express orders, it is the opinion of this Board, that it is not in their power to comply with Mr. Benfield's request in any respect. Those claims on individuals which bear the appearance of having no connection with Government, not being sufficiently explained to enable the Board to form an opinion thereon, and the assignments of the Nabob not being admissible.

A member of the Council, then in the majority, desired this matter might be reconsidered at the succeeding Council; and when it was reconsidered, a majority voted that the resolution of the 29th May should not be confirmed, which was followed by Mr. Mackay's introducing, on the 14th June, these motions.

1ſt, That it is the opinion of the Board, " That the Nabob had a right
" to the Government ſhare of the crop in the Tanjore country, the produce
" of grain ſown during the time it was in his poſſeſſion, and that any mort-
" gages he may have given on the ſame, are good."

2d, " That a letter be written to the Raja of Tanjore, to inform him of
" the above reſolution of the Board, and to recommend to him to give Mr.
" Benfield all reaſonable aſſiſtance, in recovering ſuch debts as appear to be
" juſtly due to him from the inhabitants, as well as to reſtore to him the grain
" of laſt year which was in the poſſeſſion of his people, and ſaid to be forcibly
" taken from him.

3d, " That it be further recommended to the Raja to account with Mr.
" Benfield for the Government ſhare of the grain, in the diſtricts aſſigned to
" him by the Nabob, and ſaid to be forcibly taken from his people."

Theſe motions being ſeverally put to the vote, paſſed in the affirmative, viz.

For the Queſtion.	Againſt
Mr. Mackay,	Mr. Stone,
Mr. Jourdain,	Mr. Dalrymple,
Mr. Palmer,	Mr. Ruſſell,
Mr. Floyer,	Mr. Dawſon,
Mr. Brooke,	The Preſident.
Sir R. Fletcher,	
Mr. Stratton.	

We incloſe you a paper delivered into Conſultation the 10th June, by Mr. Dalrymple, containing a ſummary account of what had paſſed upon the ſubject, together with another paper delivered in the 17th, by Mr. Stratton, Sir R. Fletcher, Meſſrs. Brooke, Floyer, Palmer, Jourdam, and Mackay.

7th. We alſo tranſmit to you a letter we have received from the Governor, General, and Council of Bengal, with our reply thereto *.

* Theſe letters are printed in this collection.

8th.

8th. The Nabob, on the 3d June, addreſſed a letter to Sir Edward Hughes; copy whereof, together with Sir Edward's letter to us, and our anſwer, came incloſed. The Nabob's letter, which is written in Engliſh, and to which he has put his ſignature, was voted in Conſultation the 17th inſtant, to have been written purpoſely to create animoſity among the members of this Government. The Preſident then gave in the following minute.

" After ſuch a letter as that written by the Nabob to Sir Edward Hughes, " and after the ſentiments of the Preſident, expreſſed in the reply to Sir " Edward Hughes, as well as what paſſed in debate upon the ſubject, the " Preſident does hope the impropriety, nay indecency, of viſiting the Na- " bob under ſuch circumſtances, muſt ſtrike every member of the Council.

" The Preſident recommends that, agreeable to the Company's ſtanding " orders, no member of the Council do henceforth viſit, or correſpond by " writing or by meſſage, with the Nabob, or either of his ſons †."

The Preſident is more particularly induced to recommend this, as he is informed that the Nabob has been made acquainted with the proceedings of this Board; and he thinks it very improper any member of the Council ſhould be liable to the ſlighteſt ſuſpicion of divulging to the Nabob the proceedings of Government.

Your Preſident is of opinion, " that unleſs means are taken to prevent " Europeans from having connection and correſpondence with the country " Government in money matters, as well as others, your affairs will ever " be ſubject to embarraſſment."

10th. Your ſtanding orders poſitively prohibit all money tranſactions with the Country Government; but ſome members of the Council think theſe orders are no longer in force, being ſuperſeded by the Act of Parliament, which your Preſident cannot admit.

11th. The conſtant uſage of the ſervice was, that all intercourſe and correſpondence with the country powers was carried on by the Preſident alone. This ſeems to be confirmed particularly by your commands of the 22d March

† Vide Mr. Mackay's Minute in reply, on the 17th of June, printed in this collection.

1771, par. 2d and 25th; March 1772, par. 64th. But at present almost every man claims a right of such intercourse with the country powers as he thinks proper.

12th. The foregoing is the draught of a letter which I proposed to be written to you from your Administration here. But the majority of the Council not consenting thereto, I think it incumbent on me to transmit it to you, and shall add, that was I sensible any part of my conduct, since my arrival here, had been improper, I would acknowledge and endeavour to rectify it; but I am persuaded I have done *my duty* ‡, and my duty only.

13th. The execution of your orders concerning Tanjore has given infinite satisfaction to the natives in general §. The Nabob was certainly not pleased *, but I am convinced he would have acquiesced, had he not been misled by evil counsellors.

14th. The letter to Sir Edward Hughes, in which such apprehensions are expressed of danger to the Nabob's person, was not sent till a week after † the visit, which, it is pretended, gave rise to those apprehensions; and in the interval I received a visit from the Nabob's sons, with a message of compliment from their father ||. The Nabob is perfectly sensible that his whole dependence is on *your protection* ‡; and I am under no doubt that I can be on good terms with him *whenever I please*; but I think it more for *your dignity* and *interest*, that the Nabob should first become sensible of the im-

‡ The majority of his own Council, and the Governor-general and Supreme Council of Bengal, are of a very different opinion.

§ A Gentleman now in London was present at Tanjore, when the Raja was restored by Lord Pigot, in the month of April last. He declares, that the whole country, remembering the former cruelties of Tuljagee, was shocked at his restoration. The Gentleman having questioned an old man of rank and property, a native of Tanjore, how he liked the restoration of Tuljagee? The old man replied, "That it were to be much wished such a profligate *fellow* had never been re-"stored; for, says he, he is so mean in soul, and naturally such a *Barrawar*, (or *pimp*) that "he would prostitute his sister or daughter to ———, and even soon *eat beef* with him."

* We have a pretty good proof of this in the preceding papers.

† It was necessary for the Nabob to sound (by the means of others) Sir Edward Hughes, whether he would protect him, as an ally of Great Britain, before he made his application in form.

|| A piece of mere *Eastern politeness* without any meaning.

‡ Yet his Highness appeals from the Company to the justice of the King, Parliament, and Nation.

propriety

propriety of his conduct, in placing his trust in men who have as little regard for *his interest* as they have for *yours* †.

I will go on as I have begun, strongly recommending every measure that appears to me proper, and resolutely maintaining, that nothing shall be done which, in my opinion, may involve your affairs in difficulty.

A majority of the Council having rejected the preceding letter, the following caution against it was written to the Company.

Extract of a Letter from the Governor and Council of Fort St. George, dated the 22d June 1776.

THE letter now transmitted by the President having been *proposed* by him, to be sent from the Board, was *rejected* by a majority of *seven* to *four*, for reasons which will appear upon the records. We hope you will *pass no opinion* upon the subjects of that letter, until you receive the whole proceedings; which will be sent by the next conveyance.

In the year 1762, Mr. George Pigot having, for reasons best known to himself, taken an affection to the interests of *Pretaupa* or *Pertaub Sing*, Raja of Tanjore, resolved to make a treaty between that Zemindar and his feudal Lord, the Nabob of Arcot. To pave the way for the treaty, a Company's servant was sent to Tanjore by the Presidency at Madras; and the Nabob finding, upon his return, that the conditions proposed to be granted to his feudatory, were highly prejudicial to his *rights* and *interests*, wrote the following letter.

Translation of a Letter from his Highness the Nabob to Governor Pigot, dated 24th Zehige 1175, or 17th July 1762.

ON the 21st Zehige, Mr. Du Pré arrived here from Tanjore, by whose representation, I understand, that the Raja of Tanjore had *verbally*

† It is difficult to say, whether his Lordship means those whom he calls *rascals* in *India*, or others *here*, whom he has been pleased in his conferences to dignify with the same *honourable appellation*.

‡ agreed

agreed to ſettle money matters. The ſums, you will be informed of by Mr. Du Pré's letter, are according to the following conditions.

Firſt, That I ſhould give the Raja a full diſcharge for what has been ſettled to the end of 1172 Fuſly. You and I wrote to the Raja in the year 1171 Fuſly; and Mr. Du Pré went in the ſame year to Tanjore. The Raja delayed the negotiation for that year. It is now but two days that the year 1172 Fuſly is begun, and there are twelve months of it to come; yet the Raja deſires that we may not demand any money from him till this year is over.

Secondly, That the bond of ſeven lacks of rupees, which he executed to the deceaſed Nabob, and for which he is indebted as well as for the preſent tribute, ſhould be given up to him, and a diſcharge for the ſame.

Thirdly, He propoſes to engage to pay the ſtipulated ſums between the beginning of 1172 Fuſly, to the end of the 1174, making three years.

Fourthly, He requires that I ſhould give up the fort of Arnee, though even the fort of Tanjore was never given to his anceſtors; therefore, what right can he have in the fort of Arnee? The thing is this, At the time that King Alum Geer took the kingdom of Hydrobad, the Marattas, thinking that the Carnatic was without a maſter, took poſſeſſion of it. They are certainly nothing but thieves. Alum Geer flead alive Sevaw, who was father to Raja Sahow; and Sahow himſelf was put into priſon. Mahomed Caumbauſh, ſon of the King*, and the Nabob Aſud Cawn Vizier, and Zulphucaur Cawn Buxſhy were employed to expel the Marattas, and took poſſeſſion of the forts of Gingee, Vellore, &c. In the mean time King

* The word King is never given to any perſon in India except the Mogul. When the Portugueſe firſt made conqueſts in India on the Malabar coaſt, they dignified the Samoria and other Rajas with the appellation of King, on account of the reſemblance which the word *Raja* bore to *Rey* (or King); hence we read of the Kings of Cochin, Calicut, &c. whoſe kingdoms and forces were found unequal to reſiſt a few adventurers. The Portugueſe having made no conqueſts in the interior parts of Hindoſtan, thoſe Rajas never obtained the royal appellation, though infinitely more powerful than the ſouthern Rajas, ſuch as the Raja of Burdwan, Nudden, &c. In this part of the country Rajas are ſo common, that many of them are reduced from neceſſity to act a Banyans. Colly Churn (who had been condemned to work on the roads in chains for his villanies) is a Raja, and was Banyan to Colonel Champion. It would have ſounded rather odd in the army, had Colonel Champion ſaid to one of his Hircarrahs, "Go tell the *King*, my *Banyan*, that I want his Majeſty immediately to buy me a larger pair of ſhoes." The word *Pacha*, and not *Raja*, means King.

Alum

Alum Geer died; and differences arose between Alum Shaw and Bahauder Shaw. Zulphucaur Cawn, who supported the Marattas, had, on his request to Alum Shaw, the Raja Sahow released from prison. On account of the variance between the deceased King's two sons, there was no power employed to drive the Marattas out of the country, otherwise the Tanjore country would not have remained in the possession of those people. In the first place, this country belonged to the Hindoos; the Raja's ancestors possessed themselves of it by deceit. When our King took Hindostan, all the Hindoos submitted to him, and agreed to pay him tribute. Those people therefore should be under our orders, and pay us tribute. The Raja calls himself a Maratta; in what manner the Marattas treated him, I write for your information. When Ragou Zatté Sing came into this country, and took the fort of Trichinopoly from Chundah Saib, he sent a message to the Raja to pay him a Crore * of rupees, otherwise he would take from him the fort of Tanjore. The Raja agreed without hesitation to pay him a Crore of rupees; and as a hostage, gave Govinderow Suttigar, who was the manager of the Tanjore country, and Ragou Fatté Sing carried him away, and put him prisoner at Cittera. When their troops withdrew from the country, the Raja did not send even a dam of the money he had agreed to pay, and the hostage remained some years in prison. He at last bribed the guards, and made his escape in the time of the late Nabob.

Fifthly, He wants that the Coallery and Elengaur should be in his possession. The thing is this; The mound of the river is near the Coallery, whereby the Tanjore people are held in obedience; you will be informed of the situation of the mound by my letter to Mr. Du Pré, a copy of which has been sent to you. Should any variance arise, and the mound be in consequence broken down, the Tanjore people would sustain great loss; as they could not in that case have water. Subter Aly Cawn broke down this mound, reduced the country, and took possession of it, and put a garrison of fifteen hundred of his troops into Tanjore Fort, under the command of Shien Lutfulla, and looking upon the fort and country as his own, he repaired the mound.

Suppose the master of the country gives the mound into the hands of the Tanjore people, the boundaries of Tanjore, which are now eight coss from

* One million two hundred thousand pounds.

 Trichinopoly,

Trichonopoly, will be brought within one cofs of it, which would give great offence to the Zemindars and other inhabitants of the Trichinopoly country; they will fay, that fuch a thing never happened from the firft eftablifhment of the former Rajas, and that it is an extraordinary meafure, to leave the mound at this time in poffeffion of the Tanjore people. If we affign it to them by writings, how fhall we be able hereafter to withdraw it? I will give you an example. The Raja of Tanjore gave by Sunned to the Tondyman, Heranelly, &c. In the truce concluded between the French and Englifh for eighteen months, the Raja (though forbid by the Englifh and me) took the Tondyman's country from him by arms. If any attention is to be given to a Sunned, the Raja fhould return to the Tondyman, Heranelly, and other countries he took from him; as alfo, he fhould give up countries which he has, without my Sunned, taken from Malacotty and the Marawar, who are my tributaries. When I demand from them my tribute, which has been a long time due, they excufe themfelves from paying it, by faying, that the Raja has got poffeffion of their countries. He fhould give up thefe countries, that I may give eafe to the minds of the Zemindars belonging to Trichinopoly. Though he pays no regard to his own Sunnud, he fhould yet attend to the Sunnud of others. The fituation of this bufinefs, you'll be fully informed of by my letter to Mr. Du Pré, a copy of which I have fent to you.

Sixthly, The tribute which the Raja ufed to pay to the former Subahdars of Arcot, and to the deceafed Nabob, he has entirely omitted, and wifhes to fix his tribute at two lacks of rupees from the year 1173 Fufly. All the Raja's propofals are of a nature never mentioned fince the eftablifhment of Trichinopoly and Tanjore, and are fuch as can by no means be approved of. He has given no part of the tribute, &c. due for fifteen years, and amounting to above a Crore of rupees. He propofes to pay a little money this year, none the next, and a little the third: Thus it would be a matter of little difference, whether bufinefs is fettled or not. Subter Aly Cawn, and Coja Abdulla Cawn, though they had but few troops, took a large fum from the Raja. By the bleffing of God, and your fupport and affiftance, I have much more power than they had. If I have not a right to more money than they got, I ought to receive what was determined on by my father. If it is your intention to fettle this bufinefs according to the Raja's wifhes, through apprehenfion that he may join the

French

French and Dutch, you may underſtand by my letter to Mr. Du Pré, that he has agreed to do that already; what he then promiſed them he will now perform. If you do not think proper to ſend troops at preſent againſt Tanjore, we ſhall, by the bleſſing of God, hereafter find means to oblige them to pay the tribute. It is the cuſtom of this country, for the ſovereign (if the Zemindars do not pay their tribute regularly, and there is not a good opportunity to oblige them to it) to collect, when they have the power of doing ſo, the tribute and arrears at once. It was agreed on between Bumrage and me, that he ſhould pay me a tribute of ten lacks of rupees; but not finding a favourable opportunity, I did not then inſiſt on it, but received, without any condition, what money he would pay. The tribute from Bungaur Yatchum, and the Collaſtry Raja, I have received according to agreement, except fifty thouſand rupees from each, which I would not take, as their troops were employed with mine, and ſuffered much in battle, as did their Peons; but I was under no agreement to allow them that money. I write you this long letter, to ſhow, that the Tanjore people have not till now employed any mediators in their buſineſs with me, but now you are deſirous of being a mediator. According to the eſtabliſhment of the Zemindars, I cannot alter the tribute; therefore I think it proper to put off the concluſion of the preſent matters. As there is friendſhip between you and me, I write you the ſentiments of my heart. It was my intention to ſettle the buſineſs of Tanjore, and that the Engliſh troops ſhould be employed only for the important buſineſs of getting in money for the expence of the Company. I intend, by the bleſſing of God, that the remainder of the debt due to the Company (which is but trifling), ſhall be paid off in the year 1172 Fuſly. If I do not get the whole money due to me from Tanjore, what ſhall I be a gainer? If you think that we can receive the money without war, and that I ſhould quit the Raja, as I do not approve of the before-mentioned terms, and ſhould he have the benefit of your mediation, he ought agree to pay in ready money, or by bills of Buckangee, Goverdendaſs, and Ballabundar Soucars, at three or four months date, the money due to the end of 1170 Fuſly, or at leaſt to the end 1171 Fuſly. I can then give my diſcharges to the time fixed. I write you my real ſentiments, and hope that the juſtice of my claims, and my influence and my power (which are due to the aſſiſtance of the Engliſh) you will so far keep in your view, that they may not be less than that of former Subadars.

What can I say more?

Notwithstanding the remonstrances of the Nabob, he was *forced* to agree to the treaty. The injustice of the conditions, with respect to his Highness, is fully set forth in the preceding letter, but some *farther* observations upon it shall be subjoined.

Treaty with the King of Tanjore in 1762.

Fort St. George Secret Consultation, the 20*th Sept.* 1762.

A Treaty and Agreement made and concluded between Woomdatool Moollock, Serajel Dowlah Anaverde Cawn Behauder, Munsoor Jung, Nabob of the Carnatic, Pyen Gaut, and Pretaupa Sing, Raja of Tanjore, in manner following.

WHEREAS a destructive war, fomented and carried on by the French and their allies, against the said Nabob, hath for many years last past wasted and afflicted the province of Carnatic Pyen Gaut, in which war the said Nabob Annaverde Cawn Behauder hath, at length, with the assistance of his allies, proved victorious, and restored peace and tranquillity to the said Province: And whereas, at sundry times during the said troubles, the said Raja Pretaupa Sing did yield some aid and assistance to the said Nabob Anaverde Cawn, whereby, as well as by the necessary defence of his own kingdom against the French, he hath been put to great expence: And whereas, by reason of the said troubles, neither the account of Paish cash due from the said Raja to the Mogul, and payable to the Nabob of the Carnatic, nor the account of expences of the said Raja, incurred as aforesaid, have been settled or adjusted; but now, it having pleased God to restore peace to these countries by the expulsion of the common enemy, the said Nabob and the said Raja being equally desirous that the people whom God hath placed under their rule may enjoy the full fruits thereof, have mutually consented to establish a firm friendship between them; and to that end they have agreed, and do agree, to settle and adjust all accounts and matters of dispute between them in manner following; and they do faithfully promise, each for what concerns himself, punctually to perform the same.

 I. The

I. The ſaid Raja Pretaupa Sing doth hereby oblige himſelf to pay unto the ſaid Nabob Cawn Behauder the ſum of twenty-two lacks of rupees, coined in the Engliſh Eaſt India Company's mint at Fort St. George, or the value thereof in ſtar pagodas, coined in the ſaid mint, valuing the ſaid rupees at the rate of 350 for 100 pagodas, at the times and in manner following, that is to ſay,

On the day of ſigning this agreement by the ſaid Pretaupa Sing three lacks of rupees — — — — —	300,000
In the month of April 1763, five lacks of rupees — —	500,000
In the month of November 1763, five lacks of rupees —	500,000
In the month of April 1764, five lacks of rupees — —	500,000
In the month of Auguſt 1764, four lacks of rupees —	400,000
In all — — Rupees	2,200,000

And the ſaid Nabob Anaverde Cawn Behauder doth agree to accept of the ſaid twenty-two lacks of rupees, in full payment and ſatisfaction for or on account of Peiſh Caſh, and in full of all accounts and demands whatſoever, unto the 10th day of July laſt paſt; being the full term and expiration of the year of Phaſley 1171.

II. The ſaid Raja Pretaupa Sing doth hereby oblige himſelf to pay yearly, in the month of July, unto the ſaid Anaverde Cawn Behauder, or his ſucceſſor, the ſum of two lacks of Rupees, as a Peiſh Caſh or tribute to the Mogul; and foraſmuch as it hath been the uſage and cuſtom to make certain preſents to the Nabob and his principal officers, at the time of paying the annual Peiſh Caſh, the ſaid Raja doth promiſe to pay yearly to the ſaid Nabob or his ſucceſſors, at the day and time of paying the ſaid Peiſh Caſh, the further ſums of two lacks of rupees as a preſent; provided that no further ſum, either for Peiſh Caſh or Durbar Charges, be demanded of him; which ſaid two lacks, making together four lacks, ſhall be paid in rupees coined in the Company's mint, or in ſtar pagodas at the above-mentioned exchange; and the ſaid Nabob Anaverde Cawn Behauder doth agree to accept of the firſt named ſum of two lacks, in full for the annual Peiſh Caſh due to the Mogul; and alſo of the ſecond named ſum of two lacks of rupees, in full for the uſual and cuſtomary preſents or Durbar Charges; and doth hereby promiſe that he will not demand any thing more.

III. Whereas the ſaid Nabob Anaverde Cawn Behader hath in his poſſeſſion a bond given by the ſaid Raja Pretaupa Sing, unto the ſaid Nabob's late Father Anaverde Cawn Bahader, dated the 15th Moon Zehedgha Hygra 1158, for the ſum of ſeven lacks of rupees, which bond appears fair and uncancelled, and without any receipt or indorſement thereon, although the ſaid Raja Pretaupa Sing doth allege, that the ſame, or the greateſt part thereof, had been diſcharged, the ſaid Nabob Anaverde Cawn Behader, as a teſtimony of his good inclinations to cultivate a laſting friendſhip with the ſaid Raja, doth promiſe, at the time of ſigning this agreement by the ſaid Raja, will cauſe the ſaid bond to be delivered up to him to be cancelled, as if the ſame had been fully paid and diſcharged.

IV. The ſaid Nabob Anaverde Cawn Behauder doth hereby confirm unto the ſaid Raja Pretaupa Sing the full and free poſſeſſion and enjoyment of the diſtricts of Coiladdy and Clangaud, which diſtricts the ſaid Nabob did give and grant unto the ſaid Raja during the late troubles, as may appear by the ſaid Nabob's Saneds.

V. The ſaid Nabob Anaverde Cawn Behauder, having expended immenſe ſums during the late troubles, in defence of the province under his government, found it neceſſary, after the expulſion of the common enemy, to call upon the ſeveral Jemidars, Polygars, and Jaguedars, to contribute each a moderate ſum, towards reimburſing the monies ſo expended in procuring the bleſſings of the peace of which they became partakers; and amongſt others, did demand of Tremaul Row, Killidar of Arni, his reaſonable *quota*; but the ſaid Tremaul Row having obſtinately refuſed to comply therewith, and having alſo in other reſpects behaved himſelf diſobediently, the ſaid Nabob found himſelf obliged to compel him to a compliance with his demand, and did accordingly ſubdue and take the Forts of Arni and Doby Guddy, with all the Jagueer thereunto belonging, as alſo the perſon of the ſaid Tremaul Row, with his family and others. The ſaid Nabob having thus convinced the ſaid Tremaul Row, and all the world, that he can and will enforce due obedience in all who are ſubject to his government, is now equally deſirous of ſhewing to all mankind that compaſſion is ſtronger in him than reſentment. From theſe motives, as well as in condeſcenſion to the requeſt of the ſaid Raja, Pretaupa Sing, the ſaid Nabob doth hereby promiſe, that as ſoon as the ſaid Raja ſhall have ſigned this agreement, he

the

the ſaid Nabob will cauſe the ſaid Tremaul Row, with his family, attendants, and all other perſons who were taken and made priſoners at Arni, to be releaſed and ſet at full liberty. And further, that on the day the ſum of three lacks of rupees, mentioned in the firſt article hereof, ſhall be paid, he will cauſe the ſaid Tremaul Row to be put in full poſſeſſion of the whole Jagueer he poſſeſſed and enjoyed before the capture of Arni (excepting however the ſaid Fort and Doby Guddy, which the ſaid Nabob will retain in his own poſſeſſion). And provided that the ſaid Tremaul Row ſhall not at any time hereafter erect, or cauſe to be erected, any fortreſs, walled Pagoda, or other ſtrong-hold; and that he ſhall not even erect or build any wall round his dwelling-houſe exceeding eight feet high, and two feet thick; and further, that the ſaid Tremaul Row ſhall in all things behave himſelf with due obedience to the government, and pay yearly, in the month of July, unto the ſaid Nabob, or his ſucceſſors, the ſum of ten thouſand rupees; and the ſaid Raja, Pretaupa Sing, doth promiſe for the ſaid Tremaul Row, that he ſhall in all things demean and behave himſelf accordingly, and pay yearly the ſtipulated ſum.

WE George Pigot, Eſq; Governor of Fort St. George, and all the Forts and Factories, and places ſubordinate thereto, Preſident of the Council for all the affairs of the Engliſh Eaſt India Company on the Coaſt of Coromandel, and alſo the ſaid Council, whoſe names are hereunto ſigned, having greatly at heart the peace and tranquillity of the countries where the Company holds poſſeſſions, and to which they trade, ſee with great ſatisfaction the concluſion of the Treaty of Friendſhip between Nabob Woomdatoul Moolock, Serajel Dowlah, Anaverde Cawn, Behauder, Munſoor Jung, Nabob of the Carnatic, Payen Gaut, and Pretaupa Sing, Raja of Tanjore, of which the foregoing is a tranſlation; and being willing and deſirous, as much as in us lies, to eſtabliſh the friendſhip between them upon a laſting foundation, do hereby promiſe to guarantee the performance of the ſaid Treaty, being thereunto invited by both parties; and accordingly we do hereby promiſe, as far as in us lies, that in caſe either party ſhall fail in the performance of the Articles he hath hereby undertaken to perform, or any part thereof, we will to the utmoſt of our power aſſiſt the other party, to compel him who ſhall fail to fulfil his agreement, and to render due ſatisfaction for his failure therein. In witneſs whereof we have hereunto ſet our hands, and cauſed the ſeal of the ſaid Company to be affixed hereto, in Fort St. George, the 12th October 1762.

GEORGE PIGOT, &c.

Ordered, That two copies thereof be wrote in the Perſian and Maratta languages; and that one of the Perſian copies, with a Maratta and Engliſh tranſlation annexed, be executed by the Nabob, and delivered to the King of Tanjore; and that a Maratta copy, with a Perſian and Engliſh tranſlation annexed, be executed by the King of Tanjore, and delivered to the Nabob; and that the inſtrument by which the Governor and Council guarantee the ſame, with a Perſian and Maratta tranſlation be annexed to each of the parts.

The following inſtructions are ſigned and delivered to Mr. Du Pré.

To Joſias Du Pré, Eſq.

SIR,

Having well weighed and conſidered all circumſtances relative to the negociation with the King of Tanjore, the nature of the Nabob's demand, the objections made by the King, and the propoſals offered by him, the conſequences of a rupture, and the advantages of an accommodation, upon the whole we have come to a final reſolution, and have obtained the Nabob's conſent to certain articles, which we hope the King may be prevailed on to ſubſcribe to; theſe articles are digeſted in form of a Treaty, two parts thereof are delivered you here, with the one ſigned by the Nabob, the other to be ſigned by the King, if he approves it, and both ſubſcribed by us as guarantees. You are to proceed to Tanjore, and endeavour to prevail on the King to accept the terms propoſed; ſhould you ſucceed herein, in ſuch caſe, upon his ſigning that part of the Treaty which is drawn out in that intention, you are to deliver to him the other part which is ſigned by the Nabob, and receive from him the ſum of three lacks of rupees, mentioned in the firſt article of the Treaty to be paid in ready money, or you may accept Soucar bills for the ſame.

You are alſo to receive from the King of Tanjore in ready money or Soucar bills, five lacks of rupees, which he offered as a preſent. This ſum is not mentioned in the Treaty, becauſe it is not the cuſtom in tranſactions between the

the Indian powers, to mention in public writings the ſums given as preſents. Of the ſaid ſum the Nabob has conſented to diſtribute amongſt the King's principal officers, one lack for their uſual cuſtom, called Datraihy, and the remaining four are to be placed to the credit of his account with the Company.

By the third article of the Treaty the Nabob promiſes, that upon the King's ſigning the treaty, he will cauſe a bond, given by the King to the Nabob's late father, for ſeven lacks of rupees, to be delivered up and cancelled; the ſaid bond is incloſed, and you are to deliver it up accordingly, upon the King's ſigning the treaty, but not otherwiſe.

The Nabob alſo engages by the 5th article, that on the day of ſigning the ſaid Treaty by the King, he will cauſe Tremoul Row, late Killedar of Arni, with his family, &c. to be releaſed and ſet at liberty. Incloſed is the Nabob's order for that purpoſe, which is to be uſed accordingly.

If you ſhould not be able to prevail on the King to ſign the Treaty as it is drawn out, you are to acquaint him, that you are not empowered to make any further conceſſions or alterations; and therefore you are to take your leave and return hither.

We wiſh you ſucceſs, and are

SIR,

Fort St. George,
20th September, 1762.

Your affectionate friends,

GEORGE PIGOT, &c.

The infringement made upon the Nabob's rights, by depriving him of the province of Tanjore; the hoſtile invaſion of his other territories by Lord Pigot's orders, the inſults offered to his perſon and authority, the calumnies raiſed againſt his character, and the threatening him with impriſonment and diſgrace, *compelled* his Highneſs to give POSITIVE DIRECTIONS, for laying the following REPRESENTATION before the Court of Directors; which was accordingly done on the 11th day of February 1777.

To the Court of Directors of the United Company of Merchants, trading to the East Indies.

*The Representation of the Nabob Wau Lau Jah, Ummeer ul Hind, Omdaht ul Mulk, Ausuph ul Dowla, Unwar ul Dien Khan Behauder, Zuphur Jung, Sepoy Saulaur, Soubahdar of the Carnatic; desiring Redress of the Grievances set forth in his Highness's Letter to the Court, bearing date the 12th February 1776 *.*

THE conduct of your Governor, the Right Honourable George Lord Pigot, has been subversive of the guarantee contained in the eleventh article of the Treaty of Paris; his Lordship having treated with disrespect and insult, exposed to contempt, and in effect levied war upon his Highness, the avowed friend of the Company, the recognized and most faithful ally of Great Britain.

The patience and resignation with which his Highness has endured these injuries and indignities, though they have sullied his honour and disgraced his government in the eyes of all Hindostan, demonstrate to the world his reliance on the justice of the Company, the Faith of Treaties, and the *Protection of the King and Parliament of Great Britain.*

The numerous and repeated acts of violence, disrespect, and hostility, of which the Nabob complains, and for which he demands redress; as well as the resignation and patience with which he has borne them, and abstained from resistance; are manifest in the correspondence, by letters and conferences, between his Highness and Lord Pigot; which are ready to be produced to the Court.

Before the orders of the Court of Directors for restoring the country of Tanjore to its former Zemindar could be known, or were even suspected, by the Nabob, his Highness had given it in command to explain to the Court the unlimited extent of his friendship for the Company, and his firm reliance and dependance on the justice, protection, and support of his Majesty and the Parliament of Great Britain.

* This letter is already in the hands of the Public; being prefixed to the *State of Facts relative to Tanjore.*

The

The declarations made to the Court on his Highneſs's part, on the 13th of February 1776, have ſince been confirmed in all his letters to Lord Pigot. In theſe letters he has repeatedly called upon his Lordſhip, not to oppreſs the "old and faithful ally of Great Britain, ſinking in the whirlpool!" He has pointed out the miſinformation under which the Court of Directors had given their orders to his Lordſhip; the injuſtice of theſe orders, their bad policy, their inconſiſtency and direct breach of *former orders*, and their infraction of the National Treaty, by which his Highneſs's rights are ſecured to him and his heirs for ever. He has conjured his Lordſhip, in the name of *the King*, *the Parliament*, *the Nation of Great Britain*, to defer the carrying his orders into execution, until the Court of Directors ſhould have time to take his remonſtrances and complaints into mature deliberation, and reconſider what they, or rather a former Court, had done.

That Lord Pigot might have no excuſe for refuſing this requeſt, the Nabob offered in the mean time to fulfil all the ſtipulations made by his Lordſhip with the Raja, to pay the troops admitted by his Highneſs as a garriſon into Tanjore, to defray the expence of the Raja's houſehold, to increaſe his allowance to whatever ſum Lord Pigot pleaſed; and to depoſit the ſurplus revenues in *ſacred truſt*, not to be appropriated until the Company ſhould decide upon his right.

But every inſtance of condeſcenſion on the part of his Highneſs, has been repaid by an increaſe of perſonal diſreſpect on the part of Lord Pigot; who at length proceeded ſo far, as to threaten the Nabob with placing "a "guard of ſoldiers on his houſe; and to keep him in priſon, and in his own "power:" which obliged his Highneſs to apply to the Commander in Chief of his Majeſty's ſquadron for protection, as an inſulted ally of the King and nation, threatened with every miſchief to be apprehended from a man, whoſe power was great, who daily abuſed it, and whoſe enmity knew no bounds.

Under oppreſſions and injuries, ſuch as never before were offered to a Prince in his own dominions, the Nabob relied on the juſtice of his cauſe for redreſs; and in order to demonſtrate the rectitude of his intentions beyond the poſſibility of a doubt, his Highneſs *now* declares, that he wiſhes for nothing ſo much as a thorough inveſtigation of his rights; and in the mean time he will conſent, "that the country of Tanjore ſhall be managed "by commiſſion; that the ſubſidy for the maintenance of the Engliſh gar-"riſon ſhall be paid; the expences of the Raja's houſehold and guard "defrayed; the charges of Government borne; and the ſurplus of reve-"nues depoſited with the Crown of Great Britain in truſt, until the mat-"ter of right ſhall be decided. The commiſſion for managing the country "to conſiſt of three perſons; one to be named by his Highneſs, one by "the Raja, and a third by the Governor General and Supreme Council "of Bengal."

But the Nabob thinks himſelf bound to declare, with that candour which will ever guide him in his tranſactions with the Company, that if this friendly propoſition on his part ſhall not meet with an acceptance, he will find himſelf under the neceſſity of calling upon the guarantees of the Treaty of Paris, in the moſt ſolemn manner; and of petitioning the King and Parliament of Great Britain, to take him and his territories into their immediate protection. For his Highneſs muſt conſider the breach made upon the national guarantee, the indignities offered to his perſon, the inſults put upon his government, and the acts of hoſtility committed againſt him (if not redreſſed without delay), to be a total infringement on the friendly connection between his Highneſs and the Company.

What can his Highneſs ſay more?

London, 11th February 1777.

OBSERVA-

OBSERVATIONS.

SHOULD the Court of Directors refuse the proposition contained in the foregoing REPRESENTATION of the NABOB, their temerity could not fail to astonish the Proprietors, as much as it would the world in general. His Highness declares in express terms, that he "must consider all friendly "intercourse with the Company to be at an end the moment his proposi- "tion is rejected by them; and that he must, in self-defence, claim the pro- "tection of the King and Parliament, and petition that he may be taken, in "matters of territory, out of the hands of the Company for ever."

Is this a matter of so little importance to their constituents, that the Directors should not think the proposition worthy of their deliberation? Could they vindicate, upon any principle of policy or justice, the rejection of an offer, which, in effect, leaves the decision of the point in dispute entirely to themselves, while it provides the only possible security, that the country of Tanjore may not be ruined in the mean time, and the revenues squandered without account, check, or control?

In such a case would it be unfair to judge, that the same *hidden* motives, which first brought about and obtained the absurd and unjust orders for the restoration of Tanjore, still operated against reversing them? Nothing would have been more probable, if we were to reason from the measures which were said to have been intended to be pursued by the *leading* Directors, in respect of this business. Instead of coming to a manly investigation of the Nabob's rights, and the causes of their own errors, it was much feared recourse would have been had to shifts equally trifling, ineffectual, and uncandid. The abettors of the orders endeavoured to intrench themselves

 behind

behind mufty, *unauthoritative* records, which prove nothing but the ignorance of the *compiler*, and to avail themfelves of a *minifterial fanction*, which only tends to fhew their own want of candour and audacity, in venturing to lay an *unfair*, *partial*, and *mutilated ftate* of the cafe, before the Secretary of State, for his confideration. The *Directors* who drew it, or directed it to be drawn, knew that *lawyers* give their opinions conformable to the ftate laid before them. And the ftate of the Nabob's cafe was calculated, by mifreprefentations and mifinformations, by perverfion of fome facts, and fuppreffion of others, to *furprife* the Minifters into fuch an opinion as the *leaders* wanted, not fuch as juftice to a faithful ally required.

In vain would they endeavour to prove, as a defence of their meafures, "that the Raja of Tanjore has been called King, and exercifed rights of "fovereignty for a long time back; that the Company derived poffeffion "of lands from his Sunneds; that Mahomed Ali Cawn is not the *eldeft fon* "of his father; that the Raja was ordered by a Phirmaund of the Mogul "to pay his tribute to the Buxy of the Empire at Delhi, and not to the "Soubahdar of the Carnatic;" and many other points equally important. For it will be found, that all the arguments drawn from thence will militate againft themfelves, and demonftrate the *fuperlative ignorance of their* COMPILER, both in regard of the ancient and prefent ftate of India.

As there is reafon to think that thofe who oppofe juftice in the India-houfe lay great ftrefs on fuch-like arguments, let us confider each of thefe heads briefly.

1ft, "The Raja of Tanjore has obtained the title of King in the Company's Records," &c. This only proves, that the Company were unacquainted with the meaning of the word Raja. Till within thefe thirty years, the Company, and even their fervants abroad, were totally ignorant of the interior parts of the Mogul Empire: they were confined to the mere diftricts of the factories, and did not dare to ftir beyond the verge of their grants. At Bengal their utmoft limits did not extend two miles from the fort; and ftragglers were liable to the moft degrading infults and punifhments if they ventured beyond them. The Raja of Kiftnagur (who, by the bye, never obtained the title of King) has frequently fent back fervants of the Company flung hand and foot on a bamboo, carried on the fhoulders of black men, for ftraying out of the limits of Calcutta. *Tempora mutantur!* There are feventeen Rajas of confequence, and hundreds of no confequence, in Bengal.

Their

Their numbers are no less considerable on the Malabar and Coromandel coasts, as well as in Orixa. Do the opposing *Directors* intend to erect the hamlets of all these Hindoo dignitaries into kingdoms, and to restore to independence upon their sovereign Lord, all the reduced Rajas of Tinivelly, Madura, Travancore, Colastry, Marawar, Malcooty, Arrialore, Ramanadeporam, Warriarpollam, Shevagunge, Alienoor, Volgole, Pulnaud, &c. and to treat them with titles of royalty? A noble Lord at present styles his *creature*, or rather his *prisoner*, the Raja of Tanjore, KING; and addresses him under the appellation of YOUR MAJESTY. Every one of the Rajas above mentioned, as being of the ancient families of their districts, have a better right to appellations of distinction than the Zemindar of Tanjore; and, perhaps, if each of them had had as much *wealth* as the Raja of Tanjore, each of them would have found a *candidate for the peerage*, to take him by the hand. While the latter, in his turn, might have found a *leading Director* to patronise him, in spite of common sense, the law of nations, and the faith of treaties.

2dly, "The Company hold lands by Sunneds of the Raja of Tanjore." This only proves that the Company has been ready to accept lands *on a very bad title*, or on no title. When this Raja attempted to grant lands by Sunned to the Dutch and Danes, and to exercise rights of sovereignty, the Directors of 1766, 1767, and 1769, ordered that he should be *reduced to obedience*. But Directors sometimes degenerate!

3dly, "Mahomed Ali Chan is not the eldest son of his father."—This to be sure is a wonderful discovery! Maupheus Chan, his elder brother, lives with him in great harmony at Chepauk. Can it be ignorance that makes some Directors at this time of day encourage such a plea as this? If they have not acquired a deeper knowledge of the Mussulmen or Mogul constitution, they ought to read the Alcoran, to learn the law; or the histories of Orme and Dow, to learn the customs. What positive right of inheritance is derived from primogeniture in the East? Do the eldest born succeed once in ten times at Constantinople? Have they succeeded oftener at Delhi? By what right do the Directors endeavour to extend our laws of succession to the Eastern princes? If this is not a sufficient answer, we need not expect that the opposing Directors will deign to read the *eleventh article* of the

TREATY

TREATY OF PARIS in regard to Mahomed Ali Chan's rights, for they have ſo trodden that Treaty under foot that it is no longer *legible by* THEM.

4thly, " The Raja was directed by Phirmaund of the Mogul to pay his " tribute at Delhi, and not to the Soubah." We imagine certain Directors were not aware of conſequences when they directed the uſe of this argument; for it deſtroys their favourite Treaty of 1762, which is a direct contravention of the Mogul's Phirmaund. Beſides, it grants what they wiſh to deny; *viz.* That the Raja is not, nor was a great and independent ſovereign, but an humble tributary, obedient to the Mogul's Phirmaund, as we have all along contended. As for the Phirmaund itſelf, it only proves, that the Soubahdar of the Carnatic at the time was refractory, and did not account for his tributes to the Mogul; no unuſual circumſtance in that empire. This Phirmaund however did not continue long in force, for the Raja of Tanjore's tribute was afterwards either paid, or compelled to be paid, to the ſubſequent Soubadars, Ally Dooſt Chan, Subter Ally, and Anwar-ul-Dien Chan the Nabob's father.

If Phirmaunds neverthelefs have ſo much weight with *ſome* Directors, why do they not give their proper weight to thoſe Phirmaunds of the Mogul which ceded the ſovereignty of the *entire Carnatic* to Mahomed Ali Chan, and his ſucceſſors for ever, in the year 1765; when we obtained Phirmaunds for the Circars and for the Dewanny of Myſore, which laſt involved the Nabob in a ruinous war, in which the Company were principals, though they *compelled* his Highneſs with their *wonted equity* to pay the whole expences. A debt from which he has ſcarcely been able as yet to extricate himſelf.

The attempt made by the oppoſing Directors to ſcreen themſelves under the indefinite anſwer of the Secretary of State, that " he ſaw nothing contrary " to Treaty in the papers laid before him," will prove equally inſufficient to excuſe them to their conſtituents for the dilemma into which they have brought them.

The papers laid before the Secretary of State for his conſideration, were *not* a fair ſtate of the caſe. The inſtrument by which Lord Pigot was appointed Governor of Madras, and that by which Mr.

Wynch

Wynch was removed, are moſt curious ſpecimens of arrogance, injuſtice, impolicy, and groſs miſrepreſentation of facts: Papers deſignedly calculated to miſlead the judgment of Adminiſtration. But his Majeſty's miniſters were cautious, and would give no opinion on ſuch authorities. The Secretary of State alone ſaid, that " he ſaw nothing contrary to Treaty." But before certain Directors aſked the authority of his Majeſty's miniſters for what came ſo directly under the national guarantee, they ſhould have laid before them a full recital of every act and tranſaction from the Treaty of Paris to the date of their Orders relative to the reduction and reſtoration of Tanjore. They ſhould have ſtated, " That the year before the peace of Paris, Mr. Pigot, as mediator between the Nabob and Pertaub Sing, Raja of Tanjore, framed a Treaty, by which Pertaub Sing, as tributary to the Nabob, agreed to pay annually four lacks of rupees, and to perform feudal ſervices: That the Nabob was very averſe to this Treaty, becauſe Pertaub Sing, as well as former Rajas, had paid larger tributes to former Soubahdars: That when this Treaty was ſigned, the Nabob had not the *power* of diminiſhing the tribute, or releaſing the Raja from any part of his feudal ſervices to the MOGUL, whoſe Governor, for the time being, he *then was*; for his Highneſs did not obtain his *independent hereditary rights* till the year after, nor the Mogul's Phirmaund till three years after: That immediately after the ratification of the Treaty, and even before Lord Pigot left the Preſidency, Pertaub Sing entered into conſpiracies againſt his ſovereign Lord, particularly with Iſouf Cawn, the rebel of Madura, whom he, as well as Tuljagee his ſucceſſor, ſupported, not only with their own troops, but alſo with a body of French whom they entertained in their pay." See Appendix to the State of Facts, No. III. " That Tuljagee, on the death of his father, aſſumed the government, without the concurrence of his feudal ſuperior: That upon every occaſion he manifeſted the utmoſt hatred to the Engliſh and to the Nabob: That he refuſed all his feudal ſervices when called upon to aſſiſt againſt Hyder Ally: That he gave Hyder aid, both in money and proviſions, which enabled him to carry the war even to the gates of Madras: That he withheld his tribute at the ſame time: That, inſtigated by Hyder, he carried fire and ſword into the Nabob's dominions, attacking the Zemindars of the Marawar, Malcooty, and Ramanadeporam diſtricts, and committing the moſt ſavage cruelties, and moſt unprovoked depredations in thoſe countries, notwithſtanding the remonſtrances and threats of the Governor and Council of Madras: That the Court of Directors seeing that the peace of the Carnatic could never be secure while the different Zemindars and Polygars remained unreduced, gave orders to assist the Nabob (by their letter 4th March 1767) in the necessary work of enforcing their obedience: That these orders were strongly reiterated in 1769: That in consequence of these repeated orders, all the rebellious Zemindars and Polygars were reduced to obedience, except the Zemindar of Tanjore, who being the most powerful, continued his disobedience the longest, and at last entered into so many conspiracies and plots against his master, that it became a measure of self-defence to attack him: That the Governor and Council, in compliance with the positive orders of the Court of Directors, particularly those dated the 17th March 1769, prepared an army to attack Tanjore, having first solemnly debated in Council the conduct of the Raja, and the infraction on the Treaty of 1762, which they pronounce to be *null and void*; first, because it extended, and indeed could extend, no farther than the life of Pertaub Sing; and, secondly, because (had it extended to Tuljagee) it *ceased to bind*, when Tuljagee *drew the sword and invaded the neighbouring districts of the Carnatic*: That his Majesty's Minister Plenipotentiary not only approved of the war, but offered the aid of his Majesty's marine forces, to carry it on: That his Majesty *congratulated* the Nabob on the success of the expedition: That the Nabob's lenity was such, that he spared the Raja, and raised the siege, on his acknowledging his offences, promising to pay up his arrears of tribute, defray the expences of the war, and offend no more: That the army had scarcely retired out of sight of Tanjore, when the Raja entered into fresh conspiracies, inviting the Marattas, the French, the Dutch, and Hyder, all at the same time, to invade the Carnatic: That the Nabob was obliged to buy off the Marattas with a heavy chout, who had actually invaded his country in consequence of the Raja's invitation: That Mr. Mostyn, the Company's president at Poonah, advised the Governor and Council of Madras of the hostile intentions of the Raja: That his correspondence with foreign powers to introduce them into Tanjore, thereby endangering the peace of the Carnatic, and the security of the Company's possessions, had been *intercepted*: That in consequence of all these intrigues, the several powers the Raja had solicited, had all assembled troops for invading the Carnatic; the French at Mauritius, the Dutch at Ceylon and Negapatnam, longeſt, and at laſt entered into ſo many conſpiracies and plots againſt his maſter, that it became a meaſure of ſelf-defence to attack him: That the Governor and Council, in compliance with the poſitive orders of the Court of Directors, particularly thoſe dated the 17th March 1769, prepared an army to attack Tanjore, having firſt ſolemnly debated in Council the conduct of the Raja, and the infraction on the Treaty of 1762, which they pronounce to be *null and void*; firſt, becauſe it extended, and indeed could extend, no farther than the life of Pertaub Sing; and, ſecondly, becauſe (had it extended to Tuljagee) it *ceaſed to bind*, when Tuljagee *drew the ſword and invaded the neighbouring diſtricts of the Carnatic*: That his Majeſty's Miniſter Plenipotentiary not only approved of the war, but offered the aid of his Majeſty's marine forces, to carry it on: That his Majeſty approved the expedition, and wiſhed the Nabob ſucceſs in it: That the Nabob's lenity was ſuch, that he ſpared the Raja, and raiſed the ſiege, on his acknowledging his offences, promiſing to pay up his arrears of tribute, defray the expences of the war, and offend no more: That the army had ſcarcely retired out of ſight of Tanjore, when the Raja entered into freſh conſpiracies, inviting the Marattas, the French, the Dutch, and Hyder, all at the ſame time, to invade the Carnatic: That the Nabob was obliged to buy off the Marattas with a heavy chout, who had actually invaded his country in conſequence of the Raja's invitation: That Mr. Moſtyn, the Company's preſident at Poonah, adviſed the Governor and Council of Madras of the hoſtile intentions of the Raja: That his correſpondence with foreign powers to introduce them into Tanjore, thereby endangering the peace of the Carnatic, and the ſecurity of the Company's poſſeſſions, had been *intercepted* †: That, in conſequence of all theſe intrigues, the ſeveral powers the Raja had ſolicited, had all aſſembled troops for invading the Carnatic; the French at Mauritius, the Dutch at Ceylon and Negapatnam, while Hyder was prepared, and the Marattas, as above mentioned, had actually entered the country. Since the reduction of Pondicherry, the Engliſh intereſt had never been in ſo critical a ſituation in India: That at a criſis ſo alarming, the Nabob had applied to the Governor and Council of Madras, repreſenting the *fatal conſequences* of any further forbearance to his vaſſal, and requeſting the aid of the Company to *diſpoſſeſs the Raja of Tanjore*:

† They ought to have laid the intercepted letters before the Miniſtry, for authentic copies were in the India Houſe.

That upon mature deliberation, it appeared to the Governor and Council, that the Raja of Tanjore had broken through *every article of the Treaty* 1762; and therefore, that they had *unanimously* concurred in a vote for undertaking an *immediate expedition against Tanjore*, in obedience to the orders of the Court of Directors, for *granting the Nabob such assistance for the reduction of his tributary, as his Highness should deem necessary for the dignity of his government*: That the Nabob had done nothing but by *agreement*, *solemnly ratified* by the Governor and Council of Madras, acting under the orders of the Court of Directors: That agreements so made and ratified, *under the seal of the Company, in council, at* MADRAS, were as valid as agreements under the seal of the Company in LEADENHALL STREET: That the Nabob had fulfilled all the articles of agreement on his part, with the utmost *punctuality* and *fidelity*: That he had incurred great expences by the expedition, and that the Company had derived great benefits from it: That the repose of the Carnatic was *secured* by the possession of Tanjore, and would be *endangered* by restoring it to the Raja, who had forfeited all right to it: That the fate of war had given the Nabob the *absolute and irrevocable* POSSESSION of it: The then *leading Directors* should have stated all these matters to the Secretary of State, and they should have furnished him with faithful extracts of every thing on their records relative to the independent rights of the Nabob, and copies of all their own contradictory orders, before they ventured to ask his opinion on the mutilated papers laid before him. Having done none of these things, their attempt to *surprise* administration into a sanction of their own breach of the national guarantee, was not only unpardonable, but an insiduous attempt to justify their own *predeterminations*, by with-holding the proper lights from the Officer of State, under whose authority they meant to shelter themselves. But the answer which they got from the Secretary of State, with the *total silence* of the other ministers to whom they applied, will not save them from being *responsible** for the consequences in which they have involved their constituents, whether those consequences may ultimately lead to the absolute loss of their territorial connections, or the loss of the

* The Court of Directors cannot plead ignorance on this point, because in their letter of March 23d, 1770, Par. 33d, they thus express themselves, "We cannot think it prudent, or ourselves "warranted, again to alarm the inhabitants of India by attempts of this nature, more especially "as perhaps we might thereby involve ourselves in the very disagreeable necessity of *answering at* "*some future period for the infraction of a public Treaty, and the consequences thereof.*"

 400,000 l.

400,000 l. granted as a free gift to the Company, exclusive of the damages which the Nabob *may recover in the courts of law.*" All these things, together with its *never* being the intention of the Court (till the thing was proposed by Lord Pigot), were so well known to several Directors, and impressed so strongly on their minds, that they refused to sign the orders.

Whoever attentively peruses the STATE OF FACTS with its *Appendix* and the *Original Papers* NOW published, will clearly see the antient and uniform subjection of the Tanjore district to the power of the Mogul's empire. But, as some men lay great stress upon the Treaty of 1762, of which they say the Company is guarantee, it is worth while to consider the Nabob's rights by virtue of that Treaty, abstracted from all others; for, it is to be presumed, the guarantee of the Treaty extends to both the contracting parties, the Nabob as well as the Raja; unless, as the Nabob has well expressed himself in his letter of the 12th February 1776, to the Court of Directors, they really construe a guarantee to be a "protection to an enemy against a friend, and not a protection to a friend against his enemy."

By this Treaty it appears, that the Company were bound as guarantee, invited by both parties; "In case either party shall fail in the performance "of the articles he hath hereby undertaken to perform, or any part there-"of, to assist the other party to the utmost of their power." It appears also by this Treaty, that it was not a league between equal powers, but between a feudatory and his master; for the Treaty recites, that "by "reason of the said troubles (the war with the French), the account of peis-"cash or tribute due to the Mogul *, and payable to the Nabob of the "Carnatic, had not been adjusted;" and lastly it appears from the Court of Directors themselves, as well as from the records of Madras, that the Raja infringed *all* the articles of this Treaty, by repeated acts of hostility and open war, which drew a positive order from the Court of Directors in 1769, to "give the Nabob such support as might be effectual, and to pur-"sue such measures as the Nabob might think consistent with the justice "and dignity of his government."

* The Nabob, as is already mentioned, has since acquired these rights *in sovereign perpetuity* for himself and his heirs.

In consequence of these premises, the Nabob declared war *regularly* against the Raja of Tanjore, the aggressor; and the Company's army marched under the orders of General Smith, to aid the Nabob or *allies*, by virtue of the guarantee; and "to proceed against the Fort of Tanjore *to* "*reduce it*; and having done so, to put his Highness's son, or any other "person authorized by his Highness for that purpose, in possession of it; "together with the military stores and effects that might be found therein."

Let us now consider the Nabob's rights after a solemn declaration of war.

One of the Directors is a lawyer, he ought to have been acquainted with the law of nature and of nations; or he should at least have paid some attention to the opinion of Mr. Du Pré, who was employed in framing the Treaty of 1762, who understood these laws perfectly, and expressed himself clearly. He writes to the following purport to the Nabob on the 25th of September 1771. "The part I take in these transactions is not as *a Principal*, "it is in support of your government and pretensions, and partly as guarantee "of the Treaty of 1762. In consequence thereof, *whatever shall be taken from* "*the Raja of Tanjore, and that shall fall into my hands, possession, or power,* "*whether forts, countries, money, effects, or military stores whatever, it shall be* "*left at your disposal,* as was done in the case of Alienoor, Worriorpollam, Vol-"gole, and Pulnaud; and in respect to the Raja of Tanjore and his family "and dependants, as your clemency and humanity are well known, I shall "leave them at your disposal; but it is necessary to inform your Excel-"lency, that, according to the *usage of war*, the plunder of places taken "by storm, is deemed the right of the captors; such plunder therefore I "have no power over, or right to dispose of."

But if it did not consist with the dignity of the *then* leading Director to consult a servant of the Company, though an able one, he ought to have taken the trouble of perusing the best writers on these laws, before he ventured to involve his constituents in a direct and obstinate breach on the Treaty of 1762. Had he consulted these writers he would have found, "that peace may be broken three ways; 1st, By doing what is contrary to "all peace. 2dly, Contrary to that which is expresly mentioned in "Treaties. 3dly, Contrary to that which is to be understood from the na-

" ture of every peace." Grot. de Bello et Pace, B. 3. Ch. 20. Sect. 27. Tuljagee broke the peace of 1771, as his father had done the Treaty of 1762, in all these modes.

" If either party *break* the leagues, the other *is freed*, because each article " of the league has the force of a condition." Puffendorf. B. 3. Ch. 8. Grot. B. 2. Ch. 15. Sect. 15. Grot. B. 3. Ch. 8. Sect. 8. Budæus de contraventionibus Fæderum, Ch. 3. Sect. 14.

" There are three ways of securing a man's self from him who injured " him: 1st, By putting him to death; 2dly, By putting it out of his power " to do him any further injury; and lastly, By the severity of his punish- " ment, to deter him from offending any more." Grot. B. 2. Ch. 10. Sect. 8. Of these three modes allowed by the law of nature and of nations, the Nabob chose the mildest (Vide the account of the first siege); but he was afterwards compelled to take the second as more effectual. His Highness never put an offender against himself, to death. He delights not in blood, but excels in mercy.

" As many sources as there are of judicial actions, so many causes may " there be of war; for, when the methods of justice cease, war begins. " Most men assign three just causes of war; *Defence*, the *recovery* of what's " our own, and *punishment*. Omnia quæ defendi, repetique et ulcisci fas " est." These three causes were united in the Nabob's war against the Raja of Tanjore, *self-defence*, the *recovery* of the tribute withheld, and *punishment* of this double delinquency. The Roman heralds denounced war against their tributaries, " because they had not given, paid, nor did, what " they ought to have given, paid, and done." Liv. as cited by Grot. B. 1. Ch. 1. Sect. 2.

" The causes of war may be reduced to three heads: 1st, To *defend* our- " selves and properties against others who design to do us harm, either by " assaulting our persons, or taking away or ruining our estates: 2d, To " assert our *rights*, when others who are *justly obliged*, *refuse to pay them to us*; " and lastly, to recover *satisfaction* for damages we have injuriously sustain- " ed." Puffend. B. 8. Ch. 6. Sect. 3.

" By

"By the laws of nations, not only he who makes a war for a juſt cauſe, "but every man in a ſolemn war, *acquires the property of what he takes from "the enemy, and that without rule or meaſure, ſo that both he and his aſſigns are "to be defended in the poſſeſſion of them by all nations*." Plato de Legibus, Lib. 1. Ariſtotle de Repub. Lib. 1. Cap. 4. Xenoph. de Inſt. Cyr. Lib. 7. Cap. 5. and Grot. B. 3. Ch. 6. Sect. 2.

"By the laws of war, all things are *lawful to the conqueror*; therefore, "the Achæans (Livy) thus addreſs the Roman Senate: How ſhould what has "been acted by the rights of war now come into debate?" Grot. B. 3. Ch. 4. Sect. 3. May not the Nabob venture to ſpeak to the *Court of Directors* what the Achæans were permitted to ſay to the *Senate of Rome*?

"Sovereignty may be acquired by *conqueſt*, either ſo far as it was in the "King or another Governor, and then *all power he had paſſes to the* CON-"QUEROR, and no more." Or as it is in the people, and then the *Conqueror has the ſame right to alienate it* as the people had; and thus *kingdoms become patrimonial.* Grot. B. 3. Ch. 8. Sect. 3.

By what has been ſaid, and by theſe extracts from the Law of Nature and of Nations, which *men* who are diſpoſers of kingdoms, ought to have known, it is clear that the Raja of Tanjore broke the peace and infringed the Treaty of 1762; that he firſt drew the ſword againſt the Nabob; that the Nabob declared war ſolemnly againſt the Raja,[a] and called upon the Company's aid, in virtue of their *guarantee* of the ſaid Treaty; that the Company gave their aid as *auxiliaries*; that the Nabob *conquered* his enemy, and became poſſeſſed of *his perſon, territories, and effects*; that by the *laws of war* he had a right to diſpoſe of all theſe *acquiſitions by conqueſt*; that the guarantees of the Treaty of 1762 had no right to deprive his Highneſs of theſe *acquiſitions by conqueſt*; that the attempt to deprive him of them is an infringement on the Treaty in 1762; that the infringement on this Treaty is alſo an infringement on the national guarantee in the eleventh article of the Treaty of Paris; and, laſtly, that this breach on the national guarantee, unleſs immediately remedied, muſt infringe the friendly connection between his Highneſs and the Company, and involve the Company in all the conſequences of ſuch infraction. What thoſe conſequences may be, will then reſt with the JUSTICE of the KING and PARLIAMENT to determine, agreeable to the Faith of Treaties and the Law of Nations!

THE END.